cooking
spanish

cooking
spanish

whitecap

contents

simple and satisfying page 6

tapas traditions page 10

Discover the delightful dishes to be found in every tapas bar in Spain; the perfect accompaniments to good conversation and a chilled glass of beer or wine.

the coastline page 54

Spain's extensive coastline has given rise to countless dishes, which range from elaborate stews such as the Catalan zarzuela to the deliciously simple, moreish fried fish of Andalusia.

plains and mountains page 98

Turn off the main roads and head for the countryside — here you will encounter the earthy, gutsy and honest home cooking that has characterized Spain for centuries.

pastries and sweets page 154

Every region of Spain has its own sweet specialities, many of which are closely linked to the seasons, religious festivals or the Moorish occupation of the country.

index page 190

simple and satisfying

The last ten years or so have seen a culinary revolution taking place in Spain. But as much as we may admire Spain's new wave of cooking, la nueva cocina, deep in the heart and not so deep in the palate lies a yearning for the earthy, gutsy and blatantly honest home cooking that you find right across the country. These traditional cuisines are the results of geography, history and personality. You will note that the plural is used — cuisines — and that is because Spanish food differs markedly from end to end and side to side of the Iberian Peninsula. As it should: that peninsula stretches north to south, from France to Africa, and east to west, from the Mediterranean to the Atlantic. A brief circumnavigation of the peninsula reveals something of the history of its ingredients and dishes.

The cooking of the northeastern corner of Spain, the Basque countries, is heavily influenced by its geography. In the Basque capital, San Sebastían, you will find some of the best seafood in Spain — from both the Mediterranean and the Atlantic — as well as the famed vegetables of Navarra and, from across the French border, foie gras from the Landes and truffles from the Périgord. One ingredient can be directly sourced to the Basques, and that is bacalao, salted and dried cod. Intrepid Basque whalers first brought bacalao back from the Canadian Newfoundland coast one thousand years ago.

Moving south and east into Catalonia, the influence of the French neighbours can be detected — for instance, in dishes where chicken liver pâté, mousse de fetge, is used — but so too can that of the Moors. Catalans share, with other northerners, a love for cooler climate rustic dishes using beans and sausage, such as garbanzos (chickpeas) with chorizo, mostly deriving from pre-Moorish times, and springing from villages of farmer peasants. Of definite Moorish origin is the introduction of rice, the basis for hundreds of dishes, only one of which is paella. This famous dish originated in the Catalan-speaking province of Valencia and consisted of rice, vegetables and chicken, frogs or snails. These days, paella often also features fish and seafood caught off the Catalan coast.

Travel inland to the capital, Madrid, and you encounter the harsh and beautiful landscape of the South and North Mesetas (plateaus). Here, you enter the realm of roast suckling pig and lamb and the cocido Madrileño, a slow-cooked stew of garbanzos (chickpeas) and meat. The North Meseta is covered in wheatfields, forests of pine, beech and oak, and grazing flocks of merino sheep. The harsher South Meseta is the landscape of Don Quixote, and is the home of the wild boar and the Manchego sheep, as well as vineyards and wheatfields.

RECORTES

Back on the eastern coast, from Murcia to Andalusia, the major influences are the Moorish past and the sea. In the case of Andalusia, the sea refers to both the Mediterranean and the Atlantic. Here, numerous seafood dishes, like sardinas Murciana and calamares a la plancha, reveal the importance of the bounty from the Mediterranean. Spain's famous cold soups — gazpacho, salmorejo, porra and ajo blanco — also derive from these hot southern regions.

It is here in Andalusia that the rich heritage of the Moorish occupation is most in evidence. The Arabs brought with them not just food but a culture. Their reign, from 711 to 1492, coincided with the highest point of Islamic civilization, and their impact on Spanish architecture, agriculture, music, landscape gardening and gastronomy is still evident some five hundred years after their departure. It is hard to imagine a Spain without oranges, roses and saffron, all gifts of the Moors.

Inland and to the north, we come to the Andalusian region of Huelva, home of the famous lamb stew, caldereta del condado, and the even more famous pata negra, the black Iberian pig. The pig in all its forms is the basis of the cuisine of Extremadura, Spain's westernmost and most isolated province, whose border with Portugal is also a culinary influence.

The seafood province of Spain is Galicia, nestled in the country's cool and rainy northwestern corner. From here come dishes such as pulpo gallego (boiled octopus) and delicacies like percebes (goose barnacles). Heading east along the Cantabrian coast, we come to the mountainous province of Asturias, home to the most famous sausage and bean dish of all, fabada Asturiana. Among the mountains known as the Picos de Europa, some of the world's finest blue cheeses are made, including Cabrales and Picon. Last, but certainly not least, on our culinary journey is the rugged and fertile northeastern province of Navarra. The rivers of this mountainous province teem with trout and salmon. The region is also famed throughout Spain for its vegetables, particularly asparagus and the local red capsicum (pepper) — el pimiento del piquillo.

On this voyage around the peninsula, we have forgotten one vital contribution to the cuisines of Spain: the Spanish character. Divided by distance, language and background, the Spanish are united by their love of good food, good wine and conversation. Out of these qualities springs the tapas tradition. The recipes in this book have been organized into sections based either on the Spanish way of life — tapas traditions and pastries and sweets — or on the country's geography: the coastline and plains and mountains. Along the way, you will become acquainted with the techniques, ingredients and influences that make Spanish dishes some of the most fascinating and varied in Europe.

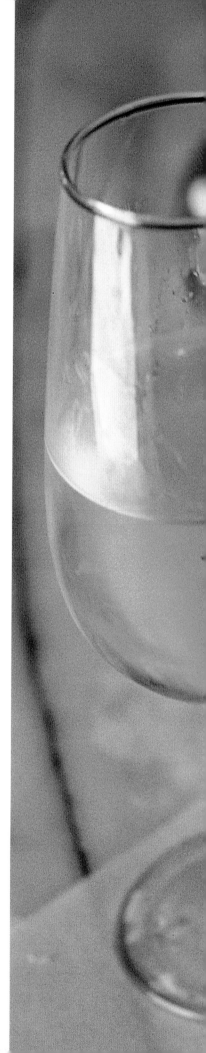

tapas traditions

In even the most ordinary tapas bar (or tasca) in a small town or one of the outer barrios (suburbs) of a large town, you are able to choose from a dazzling array of tapas. Laid out along the bar behind a glass case will be piles of black mussels, curls of garlicky prawns and shimmering stacks of sardines. Hanging overhead are succulent legs of jamón serrano (cured ham), strings of sausages, chillies like firecrackers and plump red dried capsicums (peppers).

Without a word of Spanish, you can order by pointing at such dishes as gambas al ajillo, sizzling clay pots of prawns cooked in olive oil and immoral quantities of garlic, and chorizo en sidra, a speciality from the mountainous northern province of Asturias. If you have any room, a slice of tortilla is as Spanish, as earthy and as rich as flamenco.

However, there is much more to tapas than an array of alluring dishes. Generally eaten standing up, tapas is a way of life as much as a way of eating, a convivial way to fill the gap between the end of work and the beginning of the evening meal; a leisurely stroll with friends, from bar to bar, sipping tiny glasses of chilled fino (sherry) or beer between delicious mouthfuls. Tapas is the fast food of the gods.

In the beginning, tapas were free snacks handed out by the innkeepers of Andalusia, in the country's south, with the evening glass of chilled sherry or wine. Nothing elaborate, just a slice of chorizo sausage or Manchego cheese on a hunk of coarse bread. Stop for a glass of wine or a beer in a bodega (inn) or bar in Andalusia today, and chances are you will be given such a snack.

The noun tapas is from the verb tapear (to cover), alluding to the old Andalusian habit of covering the glass with a slice of sausage or ham. Today, the habit of wandering from bar to bar is known in the south of Spain as tapeando, literally, 'tapasing'. In the northern Basque country, tapas are called pinchos (skewers), for the simple reason that many northern Spanish tapas are skewered, and the tapas crawl is known as the chiquiteo or, in the Basque language, txikiteo.

But wherever you find it, the tapas bar will be packed with locals arguing about politics and football as they eat and drink. Go in for a drink or a coffee, or both, and then stay for as long as you like, watching the passers-by, brushing up on your Spanish, listening to the old men in the corner passing conversation around the table carefully, as though it were a precious vessel — and in Spain, it is: Miguel de Unamuno, philosopher, poet, novelist and critic, wrote that 'Spanish culture is to be found in the cafés more often than the universities'.

chilli olives

. . . . fills a 1 litre (35 fl oz/4 cup) jar

IN EVERY BAR IN SPAIN YOU WILL FIND BOWLS OF OLIVES, GREEN OR BLACK, THE BEST CURED IN BRINE FOR UP TO SIX MONTHS. THIS DELIGHTFUL DISH HAS OLIVES FROM THE OLD WORLD, CHILLIES FROM THE NEW AND SPICES FROM THE EAST — A MIX OF TEXTURE AND FLAVOUR THAT WILL PLEASE THE MOST JADED OF TASTE BUDS.

garlic	3 cloves, thinly sliced
vinegar or lemon juice	2 tablespoons
cured (wrinkled) black olives	500 g (1 lb 2 oz)
flat-leaf (Italian) parsley	3 tablespoons chopped
chilli flakes	1 tablespoon
coriander seeds	3 teaspoons, crushed
cumin seeds	2 teaspoons, crushed
olive oil	500 ml (17 fl oz/2 cups)

Soak the garlic slices in the vinegar or lemon juice for 24 hours. Drain and mix the garlic in a small bowl with the olives, parsley, chilli flakes, coriander and cumin.

Sterilize a 1 litre (35 fl oz/4 cup) wide-necked jar by rinsing it well in boiling water, then leaving it to dry in a warm oven (don't dry it with a tea towel).

Spoon the olives into the jar and pour in the olive oil. Seal and marinate in the refrigerator for up to two weeks before serving at room temperature. The olives will keep for one month if stored in the refrigerator.

Spanish life and cuisine are lubricated by the juice from the fruit of the olive tree. Having arrived in Spain around 1000 BC with the Phoenicians, the olive tree was further cultivated by the Romans, but its place at the heart of Spanish cooking was really consolidated by the Moors. Today, the further south you travel, the more the landscape is carpeted with row upon row of olive trees. This is because the Moors never really made inroads into the cooler northern parts of Spain. They found the climate inhospitable, and stayed mainly in the south, as did the olive tree. Consequently, the traditional dishes of the north feature lard and butter, and those of the south, olive oil.

alcachofas en vinagreta aromática

THIS TAPA, BASED ON THE GLOBE ARTICHOKE IN A DELICIOUS SWEET-SOUR SAUCE, COMES WITH ITS OWN HANDLE, THE STALK — PERFECT FOR EASY EATING AT THE TAPAS BAR. ARTICHOKES WERE FIRST INTRODUCED INTO SPAIN BY THE ARABS IN THE MID-FIFTEENTH CENTURY, AND THEIR USE OFTEN REFLECTS THIS HERITAGE.

lemon juice	2 tablespoons
globe artichokes	4 large
garlic	2 cloves, crushed
oregano	1 teaspoon finely chopped
ground cumin	1/2 teaspoon
ground coriander	1/2 teaspoon
chilli flakes	a pinch
sherry vinegar	3 teaspoons
olive oil	60 ml (2 fl oz/1/4 cup)

Add the lemon juice to a large bowl of cold water. Trim the artichokes, cutting off the stalks to within 5 cm (2 inches) of the base of each artichoke and removing the tough outer leaves. Cut off the top quarter of the leaves from each artichoke. Slice each artichoke in half from top to base, or into quarters if very large. Remove each small, furry choke with a teaspoon, then place each artichoke piece in the bowl of acidulated water to prevent it from discolouring while you prepare the rest.

Bring a large non-aluminium saucepan of water to the boil, add the artichoke and a teaspoon of salt and simmer for 20 minutes, or until tender. (The cooking time will depend on the size of the artichoke.) Test by pressing a skewer into the base. If cooked, the artichoke will be soft and give little resistance. Strain, then drain the artichoke pieces on their cut side while cooling.

Combine the garlic, oregano, cumin, coriander and chilli flakes in a bowl. Season with a little salt and pepper and blend in the vinegar. Beating constantly, slowly and steadily add the olive oil to form an emulsion. This step can be done in a food processor.

Arrange the artichokes in a row on a platter. Pour the dressing over the top and leave to cool completely before serving.

Prepare the artichokes by removing the tough outer leaves.

Use a teaspoon to remove the furry choke from each artichoke.

jerez

We should make one thing perfectly clear right from the start. Sherry, the anglicization of Jerez (pronounced 'he-reth') is produced only in Spain, and only in what is known as the 'Sherry Triangle' — a very small segment of southern Andalusia bounded by the towns of Jerez de la Frontera, Puerto de Santa María and Sanlúcar de Barrameda, the last two situated on Spain's Atlantic coast. Anything called 'sherry' that is not produced in this region is not sherry at all, and may be a more or less pleasant imitation.

The production of sherry is a complex process: what starts out as a fairly ordinary dry white wine is aged using the solera system. Basically, a series of wines in casks, graded by age, are blended from small amounts of the oldest to larger amounts of the youngest.

If the sherry is to be a fino, its production also includes time spent under flor (flower), a growth of yeasts on the wine's surface. Finally, all sherry is fortified with brandy.

The variety and complexity of flavours of the various styles of sherry, from the steely dry fino (always served chilled) or an aged and nutty oloroso, to the lip-smacking richness of the single grape variety, Pedro Ximénez, are a revelation to those used only to the warm, sickly 'cream sherry' served by maiden aunts.

When to drink sherry? Well, in Andalusia, fino is treated as a white wine and is drunk throughout the meal — with trout or chicken, for example. Fino with oysters is another match made in heaven. But more often, it is drunk as an apéritif, simply with olives and cheese, or with tapas. The same goes for the other dry sherry, manzanilla. Like fino, it should always be served chilled — and fresh: these styles do not age well.

A dry amontillado or palo cortado is often served with soup, but the bigger, sweeter and heavier styles are best left to the end of the meal — serve the oldest and 'brownest' of olorosos or amontillados with dessert or cheese, and Pedro Ximénez with the richest of sweet dishes.

If you become a true aficionado, you will want to experiment with different sherries with every course, as is done in many modern restaurants in Andalusia.

Sherry is also used extensively in cooking, most notably in riñones en Jerez (kidneys in sherry sauce). In Andalusia, a splash of fino is often added to gazpacho.

PRODUCT OF SPAIN

Pedro

Jiménez

ACIA

A DULCE

MORILES

de Origen

para

MORILES

% vol.

chickpeas with chorizo . . . . serves 6

THIS COMBINATION OF TWO EMBLEMATIC INGREDIENTS OF SPANISH COOKING PROVIDES A SIMPLE BUT SATISFYING AND HEARTY TAPAS DISH. CHORIZO, AN OFTEN FIERY SAUSAGE OF PORK AND PIMENTÓN, IS EATEN RIGHT ACROSS SPAIN, FROM SAN SEBASTIÁN TO SEVILLE, BARCELONA TO BADAJOZ.

dried chickpeas	175 g (6 oz/³/4 cup)
bay leaf	1
cloves	4
cinnamon stick	1
chicken stock	750 ml (26 fl oz/3 cups)
olive oil	2 tablespoons
onion	1, finely chopped
garlic	1 clove, crushed
dried thyme	a pinch
chorizo	375 g (13 oz), chopped into cubes slightly larger than the chickpeas
flat-leaf (Italian) parsley	1 tablespoon chopped

Put the chickpeas in a large bowl, cover with water and soak overnight. Drain, then put in a large saucepan with the bay leaf, cloves, cinnamon stick and stock. Cover completely with water, bring to the boil, then reduce the heat and simmer for 1 hour, or until the chickpeas are tender. If they need more time, add a little more water. There should be just a little liquid left in the pan. Drain and remove the bay leaf, cloves and cinnamon stick.

Heat the oil in a large frying pan, add the onion and cook over medium heat for 3 minutes, or until translucent. Add the garlic and thyme and cook, stirring, for 1 minute. Increase the heat to medium–high, add the chorizo and cook for 3 minutes.

Add the chickpeas to the frying pan, mix well, then stir over medium heat until they are heated through. Remove from the heat and mix through the parsley. Taste before seasoning with salt and freshly ground black pepper. This dish is equally delicious served hot or at room temperature.

The chickpea, or garbanzo, is another legacy of the Moorish occupation of Spain. Though wholeheartedly adopted in that country, it was so foreign to the rest of Europe that one nineteenth-century writer could only describe it as 'a pea with an only too successful ambition to be a bean'. Chickpeas are not, as in the Middle East, crushed (to make hummus) or, as in India, ground (to make besan flour) but soaked, stewed and eaten whole. They are the most important pulse in Spain, and feature in such quintessentially Spanish dishes as olla gitana (gypsy stew) and cocido Madrileño.

albóndigas .... serves 6

ALL OVER THE WORLD YOU WILL FIND MEATBALLS, BUT NONE AS FLAVOURSOME AS THE ALBÓNDIGA OF SPAIN. ORIGINALLY MOORISH — ALL SPANISH WORDS STARTING WITH AL- ARE ARABIC IN ORIGIN — THESE MEATBALLS ARE RECOGNIZABLE THROUGH THEIR RICH SAUCE, GOLDEN-FRIED APPEARANCE AND GENEROUS USE OF SPICES.

minced (ground) pork	175 g (6 oz)
minced (ground) veal	175 g (6 oz)
garlic	3 cloves, crushed
dry breadcrumbs	35 g (1 1/4 oz/1/3 cup)
ground coriander	1 teaspoon
ground nutmeg	1 teaspoon
ground cumin	1 teaspoon
ground cinnamon	a pinch
egg	1
olive oil	2 tablespoons

spicy tomato sauce

olive oil	1 tablespoon
onion	1, chopped
garlic	1 clove, crushed
dry white wine	125 ml (4 fl oz/1/2 cup)
good-quality crushed tomatoes	400 g (14 oz) can
tomato paste (purée)	1 tablespoon
chicken stock	125 ml (4 fl oz/1/2 cup)
cayenne pepper	1/2 teaspoon
fresh or frozen peas	80 g (2 3/4 oz/1/2 cup)

Combine the pork, veal, garlic, breadcrumbs, spices, egg and some salt and pepper in a bowl. Mix by hand until the mixture is smooth and leaves the side of the bowl. Refrigerate, covered, for 30 minutes.

Roll tablespoons of the mixture into balls. Heat 1 tablespoon olive oil in a frying pan and toss half the meatballs over medium–high heat for 2–3 minutes, or until browned. Drain on paper towels. Add the remaining oil, if necessary, and brown the rest of the meatballs. Drain on paper towels.

To make the spicy tomato sauce, heat the oil in a frying pan over medium heat and add the onion. Cook, stirring occasionally, for 3 minutes, or until soft and translucent. Add the garlic and cook for 1 minute. Increase the heat to high, add the wine and boil for 1 minute. Add the crushed tomato, tomato paste and stock and simmer for 10 minutes. Stir in the cayenne pepper, peas and meatballs and gently simmer for 5–10 minutes, or until the sauce is thick. Serve hot.

Put the meatball ingredients in a large bowl and stir to combine.

Form the mixture into balls, then cook until brown all over.

Add the cayenne pepper to the spicy tomato sauce and simmer.

three ways with garlic

YOUR FIRST SMELL OF SPAIN IS GARLIC. YOUR FIRST TASTE OF SPANISH FOOD IS PROBABLY GAMBAS AL AJILLO (GARLIC PRAWNS). GARLIC IN SPAIN IS NOT USED AS A DELICATE ADDITION WITH WHICH TO FLAVOUR FOOD, BUT AS A VEGETABLE IN ITS OWN RIGHT. CUT GARLIC IS RUBBED ONTO BREAD, WHOLE CLOVES ARE THROWN INTO STEWS, GARLIC CHIPS ARE STREWN OVER FRIED FISH, AND DISHES SUCH AS SOPA DE AJOS AND AJO BLANCO ARE CHILLED SOUPS WHOSE MAIN INGREDIENT IS, OF COURSE, GARLIC.

gambas al ajillo

Preheat the oven to 250°C (500°F/Gas 9). Peel 1.25 kg (2 lb 12 oz) uncooked prawns (shrimp), leaving the tails intact. Pull out the vein from the back, starting at the head. Cut a slit down the back of each prawn. Divide 200–250 ml (7–9 fl oz) olive oil among four 500 ml (17 fl oz/2 cup) cast-iron pots. Crush 8 garlic cloves and divide half among the pots. Put the pots on a baking tray and heat in the oven for 10 minutes, or until the mixture is bubbling. Remove from the oven and divide the prawns and remaining garlic among the pots. Return to the oven for 5 minutes, or until the prawns are cooked. Stir in 2 thinly sliced spring onions (scallions). Season to taste. Serve with crusty bread to mop up the juices. Serves 4.

pan con tomate

Slice 1 crusty bread stick diagonally, and halve 6 garlic cloves and 3 vine-ripened tomatoes. Toast the slices very lightly. Rub them on one side with a cut garlic clove, then rub with half a tomato, squeezing the juice onto the bread. Season with a little salt and drizzle with extra virgin olive oil. Serve as part of a tapas or as a simple snack. Serves 6.

champiñones al ajillo

Crush 4 garlic cloves and finely slice 2 more. Finely chop 1/4 long red chilli. Finely slice 650 g (1 lb 7 oz) button, Swiss brown or pine mushrooms. Sprinkle 1 1/2 tablespoons lemon juice over the mushrooms. Heat 60 ml (2 fl oz/1/4 cup) olive oil in a large frying pan and add the crushed garlic and chopped chilli. Stir over medium–high heat for 10 seconds, then add the mushrooms. Season and cook, stirring often, for 8–10 minutes. Stir in the sliced garlic and 2 teaspoons chopped flat-leaf (Italian) parsley and cook for another minute. Serve hot. Serves 4.

gambas al ajillo

patatas bravas . . . . serves 6

THIS IS A DISH RARELY SEEN OUTSIDE THE TAPAS BAR, AND WHICH CAN, LIKE THE SIMPLE TORTILLA, REVEAL THE QUALITY OF THE REST OF THE TAPAS AT THE BAR. THE TELLTALE SIGNS OF A GOOD PATATAS BRAVAS ARE POTATOES THAT ARE FIRM TO THE MOUTH BUT NOT STARCHY, AND A SAUCE THAT IS DEEPLY SPICY.

all-purpose potatoes, such as desiree	1 kg (2 lb 4 oz)
oil	for deep-frying
Roma (plum) tomatoes	500 g (1 lb 2 oz)
olive oil	2 tablespoons
red onion	¼, finely chopped
garlic	2 cloves, crushed
sweet pimentón (paprika)	3 teaspoons
cayenne pepper	¼ teaspoon
bay leaf	1
sugar	1 teaspoon
flat-leaf (Italian) parsley	1 tablespoon chopped, to garnish, optional

Peel the potatoes, then cut them into 2 cm (³/4 inch) cubes. Rinse, then drain well and pat dry. Fill a deep-fat fryer or large heavy-based saucepan one-third full of oil and heat to 180°C (350°F), or until a cube of bread dropped into the oil browns in 15 seconds. Cook the potato in batches for 5 minutes, or until golden. Drain well on paper towels. Do not discard the oil.

Score a cross in the base of each tomato. Put in a saucepan of boiling water for 10 seconds, then plunge into cold water and peel the skin away from the cross. Chop the flesh.

Heat the olive oil in a saucepan over medium heat and cook the onion for 3 minutes, or until softened. Add the garlic, pimentón and cayenne pepper and cook for 1–2 minutes, or until fragrant.

Add the chopped tomato, bay leaf, sugar and 80 ml (2¹/2 fl oz/ ¹/3 cup) water and cook, stirring occasionally, for 20 minutes, or until thick and pulpy. Cool slightly and remove the bay leaf. Blend in a food processor until smooth, adding a little water if necessary. Before serving, return the sauce to the saucepan and simmer over low heat for 2 minutes, or until heated through. Season well.

Reheat the oil to 180°C (350°F) and cook the potato again, in batches, for 2 minutes, or until very crisp and golden. Drain on paper towels. This second frying makes the potato extra crispy and stops the sauce soaking in immediately. Put on a platter and cover with the sauce. Garnish with the parsley, if using, and serve.

Cut a cross in the tomatoes, then blanch and peel the skin away.

Cook the potato a second time in the hot oil until crisp and golden.

croquetas . . . . makes 24

THESE LITTLE DEEP-FRIED SNACKS ARE LOVED FOR THEIR SUBLIME SYMPHONY OF CRUNCHY OUTSIDE AND CREAMY INSIDE, WHICH, IF PERFECT, WILL EXPLODE IN THE MOUTH WITH RICH FLAVOUR — IN THIS CASE, OF JAMÓN.

butter	90 g (3¼ oz)
onion	1 small, finely chopped
open cap mushrooms	115 g (4 oz), finely chopped
plain (all-purpose) flour	125 g (4½ oz/1 cup), plus
	60 g (2¼ oz/½ cup), extra
milk	250 ml (9 fl oz/1 cup)
chicken stock	185 ml (6 fl oz/¾ cup)
jamón or prosciutto	115 g (4 oz), finely chopped
eggs	2, lightly beaten
dry breadcrumbs	50 g (1¾ oz/½ cup)
oil	for deep-frying

Melt the butter in a saucepan over low heat, add the onion and cook for 5 minutes, or until translucent. Add the mushrooms and cook over low heat, stirring occasionally, for 5 minutes. Add the flour and stir over medium–low heat for 1 minute, or until the mixture is dry and crumbly and begins to change colour. Remove from the heat and gradually add the milk, stirring until smooth. Stir in the stock and return to the heat, stirring until the mixture boils and thickens. Stir in the ham and some freshly ground black pepper, then transfer the mixture to a bowl to cool for 2 hours.

Roll heaped tablespoons of the mixture into croquette shapes about 6 cm (2½ inches) long. Put the extra flour, beaten egg and breadcrumbs into three shallow bowls. Toss the croquettes in the flour, dip in the egg, allowing the excess to drain away, then roll in the breadcrumbs. Put on a baking tray and refrigerate for about 30 minutes.

Fill a deep heavy-based saucepan one-third full of oil and heat to 170°C (325°F), or until a cube of bread dropped into the oil browns in 20 seconds. Add the croquettes in batches and deep-fry for 3 minutes, turning, until brown. Drain well. Serve hot.

To make the croquetas, combine the flour with the mushrooms.

Roll the mixture into croquette shapes in your hands.

Chill the breadcrumb-coated croquetas before cooking.

three ways with capsicums

THE SPANISH NAME FOR CAPSICUM (PEPPER) IS PIMIENTO. IT COMMEMORATES COLUMBUS' MISTAKEN BELIEF THAT HE WAS FORGING A NEW ROUTE TO THE EAST, THE HOME OF SPICES SUCH AS BLACK PEPPER, WHICH THE SPANIARDS CALLED PIMIENTA. THE NEW ENDING, THE MASCULINE 'O', POINTED TO THE MORE POWERFUL HEAT OF THE CHILLI PEPPER HE FOUND IN THE AMERICAS. TO CONFUSE MATTERS EVEN MORE, PIMIENTO NOW MEANS ALL FORMS OF CAPSICUM, INCLUDING THE CHILLI, WHICH IS KNOWN AS EL PIMIENTO PICANTE — HOT PEPPER.

marinated capsicums

Preheat the grill (broiler). Cut 3 red capsicums (peppers) into quarters, remove the seeds and membrane and grill (broil), skin side up, until the skin blackens and blisters. Cool in a plastic bag, then peel. Slice thinly, then put in a bowl with 3 thyme sprigs, 1 thinly sliced garlic clove, 2 teaspoons roughly chopped flat-leaf (Italian) parsley, 1 bay leaf and 1 sliced spring onion (scallion). Mix well. Whisk together 1 teaspoon sweet pimentón (paprika), 60 ml (2 fl oz/¼ cup) extra virgin olive oil, 2 tablespoons red wine vinegar and some salt and freshly ground black pepper. Pour over the capsicum mixture and toss to combine. Cover and refrigerate for at least 3 hours, or preferably overnight. Remove from the refrigerator about 30 minutes before serving. Serves 6.

spanish vegetable stew

Heat 125 ml (4 fl oz/½ cup) extra virgin olive oil in a flameproof casserole dish. Add 1 chopped large onion and cook over medium heat for 5 minutes, then add 3 finely chopped garlic cloves. Add 2 seeded and roughly diced green capsicums (peppers), 2 peeled and roughly diced zucchini (courgette) and cook over low heat for 5 minutes. Add 1 kg (2 lb 4 oz) peeled and coarsely diced vine-ripened tomatoes. Season with salt and simmer over low heat for 30 minutes, or until the flavours blend, stirring to prevent the vegetables sticking to the bottom of the dish. Serve with canned tuna or scrambled or hard-boiled eggs, or as a tapa, served on top of a slice of toasted crusty bread with an anchovy to garnish. Serves 6.

red capsicum salad

Preheat the oven to 200°C (400°F/Gas 6). Put 1 kg (2 lb 4 oz) red capsicums (peppers) in a roasting tin and rub all over with olive oil. Add 3 large unpeeled garlic cloves and 1 large beef steak tomato and cook for 15 minutes. Remove the garlic and the tomato, turn the capsicums and cook for another 15 minutes. Skin, seed and chop the tomato flesh, reserving the juice. Peel the garlic. Put the capsicum in a bag to cool, then peel, seed and slice the flesh into strips, reserving the juice. Arrange the capsicum strips on a serving dish. Pound or process the garlic and tomato to a paste. Add 80 ml (2½ fl oz/⅓ cup) extra virgin olive oil, 1 teaspoon sherry vinegar and the reserved tomato and capsicum juices and mix through. Pour the dressing over the capsicum and sprinkle with 1 tablespoon chopped flat-leaf (Italian) parsley. Serves 4.

marinated capsicums

tuna empanadas ....makes 24

ORIGINALLY FROM GALICIA, THE EMPANADA IS SPAIN'S VERSION OF THE PIE. IT WOULD HAVE BEEN A PRACTICAL AND SATISFYING SNACK FOR THE HARDY GALICIANS, WHO FOR CENTURIES HAVE BEEN FARMERS AND FISHERMEN IN A DIFFICULT LANDSCAPE. TODAY, IT COMES WITH A VARIETY OF FILLINGS, BUT THE TUNA VERSION IS A FAVOURITE.

plain (all-purpose) flour	400 g (14 oz/3¼ cups), plus extra for rolling
butter	80 g (2¾ oz), softened
eggs	3, one lightly beaten
white wine	60 ml (2 fl oz/¼ cup)

filling

olive oil	1 tablespoon
onion	1 small, finely diced
tomato paste (purée)	2 teaspoons
canned tomatoes	125 g (4½ oz/½ cup), chopped
tuna	85 g (3 oz) can, drained
roasted capsicum (pepper)	1½ tablespoons chopped
flat-leaf (Italian) parsley	2 tablespoons chopped

Sift the flour and 1 teaspoon salt into a large bowl. Rub the butter into the flour until the mixture resembles fine breadcrumbs. Combine the 2 whole eggs and the wine and add to the bowl, cutting the liquid in with a flat-bladed knife to form a dough. Turn onto a lightly floured surface and gather together into a smooth ball (do not knead or you will end up with tough pastry). Cover with plastic wrap and refrigerate for 30 minutes.

To make the filling, heat the olive oil in a frying pan over medium heat and cook the onion for about 5 minutes, or until translucent. Add the tomato paste and chopped tomato and cook for about 10 minutes, or until thick. Add the tuna, roasted capsicum and parsley and season well.

Preheat the oven to 190°C (375°F/Gas 5). Dust a work surface with a little extra flour. Roll out half the pastry to a thickness of 2 mm (1/16 inch). Using a 10 cm (4 inch) cutter, cut into 12 rounds. Put a heaped tablespoon of filling on each round, fold over and brush the edges with water, then gently pinch to seal. Continue with the remaining rounds, then repeat with the remaining dough and filling to make 24 empanadas.

Transfer to a lightly oiled baking sheet and brush each empanada with the beaten egg. Bake for about 30 minutes, or until golden. Serve warm or cold.

Use a flat-bladed knife to cut the egg mixture into the flour.

Fold each pastry round in half, encasing the filling.

Pinch the pastry edges together with your fingers, to seal.

stuffed mussels . . . . makes 18

CHEAPER AND MORE VERSATILE THAN THEIR MOLLUSC RELATION, THE OYSTER, MUSSELS LEND THEMSELVES TO A GREAT NUMBER OF PREPARATIONS, INCLUDING THIS DELICIOUSLY CRUNCHY, GARLICKY DISH.

black mussels	18
olive oil	2 teaspoons
spring onions (scallions)	2, finely chopped
garlic	1 clove, crushed
tomato paste (purée)	1 tablespoon
lemon juice	2 teaspoons
flat-leaf (Italian) parsley	4 tablespoons chopped
dry breadcrumbs	70 g (2½ oz/¾ cup)
eggs	2, beaten
oil	for deep-frying

white sauce

butter	20 g (¾ oz)
plain (all-purpose) flour	1½ tablespoons
milk	2 tablespoons

Scrub the mussels and remove the hairy beards. Discard any open mussels that don't close when tapped on the bench. Bring 250 ml (9 fl oz/1 cup) water to the boil in a saucepan, add the mussels, then cover and cook for 3–4 minutes, shaking the pan occasionally, until the mussels have just opened. Remove them from the pan as soon as they open. Strain the liquid into a jug until you have 80 ml (2½ fl oz/⅓ cup) and reserve. Discard any unopened mussels. Remove the mussels from their shells and discard one half shell from each. Finely chop the mussel meat.

Heat the olive oil in a frying pan, add the spring onion and cook for 1 minute. Add the garlic and cook for another minute. Stir in the mussels, tomato paste, lemon juice, half the parsley and some salt and freshly ground black pepper. Set aside to cool.

To make the white sauce, melt the butter in a saucepan over low heat. Add the flour and cook for about 1 minute, or until pale and foaming. Remove from the heat and gradually whisk in the reserved mussel liquid, the milk and some freshly ground black pepper. Return to the heat and cook, stirring, for 1 minute, or until the sauce boils and thickens. Reduce the heat and simmer for 2 minutes. Allow to cool.

Spoon the mussel mixture into the shells. Top each with some of the white sauce, heaping the mixture neatly.

Combine the breadcrumbs and remaining parsley on a plate. Dip the mussels in the beaten egg, then press in the crumbs to cover the top. Fill a deep heavy-based saucepan one-third full of oil and heat to 180°C (350°F), or until a cube of bread browns in 15 seconds. Cook the mussels in batches for 10–15 seconds, or until lightly browned. Remove with a slotted spoon and drain well. Serve hot.

Cook the mussels in boiling water, lifting them out as they open.

Smooth the white sauce over the mussel mixture in each shell.

three ways with meat tapas

CARNIVORES ARE WELL LOOKED AFTER IN SPAIN, WITH A WIDE CHOICE OF MEATS SERVED EVERYWHERE. GOAT IS POPULAR, AS ARE RABBIT AND HARE. IN THE TOWNS OF SEPÚLVEDA IN SEGOVIA, AND ARANDA DE DUERO IN BURGOS, FOR EXAMPLE, WHOLE STREETS ARE LINED WITH RESTAURANTS DEVOTED TO ROASTED SUCKLING PIG AND LAMB. EVEN THE FIGHTING BULLS, ONCE VANQUISHED, END UP IN THE COOKING POT. IN SPITE OF THE SPANISH FONDNESS FOR VEGETABLES, THESE TOO ARE INVARIABLY SERVED WITH MEAT, SUCH AS BEANS WITH HAM.

chorizo in apple cider sauce

Heat 60 ml (2 fl oz/¼ cup) olive oil in a saucepan over low heat. Add 1 finely chopped small onion and cook for 3 minutes, or until soft, stirring occasionally. Add 1½ teaspoons sweet pimentón (paprika) and cook for 1 minute. Increase the heat to medium, add 125 ml (4 fl oz/½ cup) dry alcoholic apple cider, 60 ml (2 fl oz/¼ cup) chicken stock and 1 bay leaf to the pan and bring to the boil. Reduce the heat and simmer for 5 minutes. Slice 280 g (10 oz) chorizo on the diagonal, add to the pan and simmer for 5 minutes, or until the sauce has reduced slightly. Stir in 2 teaspoons sherry vinegar and 2 teaspoons chopped flat-leaf (Italian) parsley. Serve hot. Serves 4.

broad beans with jamón

Melt 20 g (¾ oz) butter in a large saucepan and add 1 finely chopped onion, 175 g (6 oz) roughly chopped jamón or prosciutto and 2 crushed garlic cloves. Cook over medium heat for 5 minutes, stirring often, until the onion softens. Add 500 g (1 lb 2 oz) fresh or frozen broad (fava) beans and 125 ml (4 fl oz/½ cup) dry white wine and cook over high heat until reduced by half. Add 185 ml (6 fl oz/¾ cup) chicken stock, reduce the heat, cover and cook for about 10 minutes. Uncover and simmer for another 10 minutes. Serve warm as a tapas dish with crusty bread or hot as a side dish. Serves 4.

chicken in garlic sauce

Trim any excess fat from 1 kg (2 lb 4 oz) chicken thigh fillets and cut the thighs into thirds. Combine 1 tablespoon sweet pimentón (paprika) with some salt and freshly ground black pepper in a bowl, add the chicken and toss to coat. Heat 1 tablespoon olive oil in a large frying pan over high heat and cook 8 unpeeled garlic cloves for 1–2 minutes, or until brown. Remove from the pan. Cook the chicken in batches for 5 minutes, or until brown all over. Return all the chicken to the pan, add 60 ml (2 fl oz/¼ cup) dry sherry, boil for 30 seconds, then add 125 ml (4 fl oz/½ cup) chicken stock and 1 bay leaf. Reduce the heat to low and simmer, covered, for about 10 minutes. Meanwhile, squeeze the garlic pulp into a mortar or small bowl. Add 2 tablespoons chopped flat-leaf (Italian) parsley and pound with the pestle or mix with a fork to form a paste. Stir into the chicken, then cover and cook for 10 minutes, or until tender. Serve hot. Serves 6.

chorizo in apple cider sauce

buñuelos de bacalao

THESE EXQUISITE LITTLE FRITTERS ARE A CLASSIC CATALAN TAPAS DISH AND ARE A TESTAMENT TO THE ENDURING APPEAL OF BACALAO (SALT COD), FIRST BROUGHT TO SPAIN BY BASQUE FISHERMEN. SUCH IS THE POPULARITY OF THIS DISH THAT IT IS EVEN SERVED AS AN APPETIZER IN SOME OF THE BETTER RESTAURANTS.

bacalao (salt cod)	500 g (1 lb 2 oz)
potato	1 large, unpeeled (200 g/7 oz)
milk	2 tablespoons
olive oil	60 ml (2 fl oz/$^1/_4$ cup)
onion	1 small, finely chopped
garlic	2 cloves, crushed
self-raising flour	30 g (1 oz/$^1/_4$ cup)
eggs	2, separated
flat-leaf (Italian) parsley	1 tablespoon chopped
oil	for deep-frying

Soak the bacalao in plenty of cold water for about 20 hours, changing the water four or five times to remove excess saltiness. Cook the potato in a saucepan of boiling water for 20 minutes, or until soft. When cool, peel and mash in a bowl with the milk and 2 tablespoons of the olive oil.

Drain the bacalao, cut into large pieces and put in a saucepan. Cover with water, bring to the boil over high heat, then reduce the heat to low — it should be no hotter than 65°C (150°F) — and poach for 35–45 minutes, or until the fish is soft and there is a froth on the surface. Drain. When cool enough to handle, remove the skin and any bones, then mash the flesh with a fork until flaky.

Heat the remaining oil in a small frying pan and cook the onion over medium heat for 5 minutes, or until softened and starting to brown. Add the garlic and cook for 1 minute. Remove the pan from the heat.

Combine the potato, bacalao, onion mixture, flour, egg yolks and parsley in a bowl and season. Whisk the egg whites until stiff, then fold into the mixture. Fill a deep-fat fryer or heavy-based saucepan one-third full of olive oil and heat to 190°C (375°F), or until a cube of bread dropped into the oil browns in 10 seconds. Drop heaped tablespoons of the mixture into the oil and cook, turning once, for 2–3 minutes, or until puffed and golden. Drain well and serve immediately.

russian salad... serves 4 to 6

THIS DELICIOUS DISH OFFERS UP ONE OF THE GREAT MYSTERIES OF LIFE. WHY IS A GARLICKY POTATO AND ARTICHOKE SALAD HAILING FROM RUSSIA TO BE FOUND IN EVERY TAPAS BAR IN SPAIN? NO MATTER, IT'S AN IDEAL ACCOMPANIMENT TO A REFRESHING GLASS OF COLD BEER.

canned artichoke hearts	3
waxy potatoes, such as desiree	3, unpeeled
baby green beans	100 g (3½ oz), trimmed and cut into 1 cm (½ inch) lengths
carrot	1 large, cut into 1 cm (½ inch) dice
fresh or frozen peas	125 g (4½ oz)
cornichons	30 g (1 oz), chopped
baby capers	2 tablespoons, rinsed
anchovy fillets	4, finely chopped
black olives	10, each cut into 3 slices, plus 5 extra, to garnish

mayonnaise

eggs	2, separated
Dijon mustard	1 teaspoon
extra virgin olive oil	125 ml (4 fl oz/½ cup)
lemon juice	2 tablespoons
garlic	2 small cloves, crushed

To make the mayonnaise, use electric beaters to beat the egg yolks with the Dijon mustard and ¼ teaspoon salt until creamy. Gradually add the oil in a slow, fine stream, beating constantly until all the oil has been added. Add the lemon juice, garlic and 1 teaspoon boiling water and beat for 1 minute, or until well combined. Season to taste.

Cut each artichoke heart into quarters. Rinse the potatoes, put in a saucepan, cover with salted cold water and bring to a gentle simmer. Cook for 15–20 minutes, or until tender when pierced with a knife. Drain well and allow to cool slightly. Peel and set aside. When the potatoes are completely cool, cut into 1 cm (½ inch) dice.

Blanch the beans in boiling salted water until tender but still firm to the bite. Refresh in cold water, then drain thoroughly. Repeat with the carrot and peas.

Set aside a small quantity of each vegetable, including the chopped cornichons, for the garnish and season to taste. Put the remainder in a bowl with the capers, anchovies and sliced olives. Add the mayonnaise, toss to combine and season. Arrange on a serving dish and garnish with the reserved vegetables and the whole olives.

Add the oil to the egg yolks in a slow, steady stream.

Blanch the green beans in boiling water, then refresh in cold water.

Pour the mayonnaise over the vegetables and toss to mix.

three ways with seafood tapas

A MOONLIT WANDER IN SEVILLE, PAST GARDENS AND PLAZAS FRAGRANT WITH JASMINE AND MAGNOLIA, WILL LEAD YOU TO THE TAPAS BAR QUARTER AROUND CALLE CANO Y CUETO. HERE, YOU WILL FIND THE MOST SENSATIONAL SEAFOOD TAPAS, USING PRAWNS (SHRIMP), WHITEBAIT AND SCALLOPS, ALL FRIED TO PERFECTION. THERE ARE ALSO DISHES OF FRIED BABY EEL, LITTLE PLATEFULS OF SWEET BABY MOLLUSCS AND SEA SNAILS, WHICH ARE EATEN BY SUCKING THE FLESH STRAIGHT OUT OF THEIR HORNY SHELLS. AND THEN IT'S TIME FOR DINNER.

tortillitas de camerones

Separately sift 60 g (2¼ oz/½ cup) plain (all-purpose) flour and 55 g (2 oz/½ cup) chickpea flour, then combine them in a bowl. Add 1 teaspoon sweet pimentón (paprika) and make a well in the centre. Pour in 4 lightly beaten large eggs and mix in gradually, then stir in 60 ml (2 fl oz/¼ cup) water to make a smooth batter. Add 4 finely chopped spring onions (scallions), 4 tablespoons finely chopped flat-leaf (Italian) parsley and 500 g (1 lb 2 oz) peeled and finely chopped raw prawns (shrimp) — about 800 g (1 lb 12 oz) unpeeled — and season well. Rest for at least 30 minutes. Heat 125 ml (4 fl oz/½ cup) extra virgin olive oil or olive oil in a deep-sided frying pan over medium–low heat. Spoon in 2 tablespoons of batter per fritter and flatten into a thin pancake. Cook in batches for about 3 minutes on each side, or until golden and cooked through. Remove the fritters from the pan and drain on paper towels. Repeat with the remaining batter to make 20 in all. Season well and serve with lemon wedges. Makes 20.

calamares fritos

Wash 500 g (1 lb 2 oz) cleaned calamari tubes and cut into rings about 1 cm (½ inch) thick. Combine 175 g (6 oz/1½ cups) plain (all-purpose) flour and 2 teaspoons sweet pimentón (paprika). Season the calamari rings well with salt and freshly ground black pepper and toss in the flour to lightly coat. Fill a deep, heavy-based saucepan one-third full of extra virgin olive oil or olive oil and heat to 180°C (350°F), or until a cube of bread dropped into the oil browns in 15 seconds. Add the calamari in batches and cook for about 2 minutes, or until golden. Drain and serve hot with lemon wedges and allioli (page 48) on the side, if desired. Serves 4.

banderillas

Soak 8 wooden skewers in cold water for 1 hour to prevent them from burning during cooking. Cut 250 g (9 oz) good-quality raw tuna into 24 even-sized cubes. Remove the zest from 1 lemon, avoiding the bitter white pith, and cut the zest into thin strips. Put the tuna, lemon zest, 1 tablespoon lemon juice and 1 tablespoon olive oil in a bowl for 5–10 minutes to infuse. Using 16 caperberries and 8 green olives stuffed with anchovies in total, thread 3 pieces of tuna, 2 caperberries and 1 green olive onto each skewer, alternating each ingredient. Put the skewers in a non-metallic dish and pour the marinade over. Cook under a hot grill (broiler), turning to cook each side, for about 4 minutes, or until done to your liking. Makes 8.

tortillitas de camerones

prawns with romesco sauce

. . . . serves 6 to 8

THIS CLASSIC CATALAN SAUCE IS FROM THE TOWN OF TARRAGONA. IT IS BEST MADE WITH THE ROMESCO OR NYORA CAPSICUM (PEPPER), THOUGH ANCHO CHILLIES OR ANY DRIED CAPSICUM WILL ALSO WORK WELL. ROMESCO SAUCE IS FAMED AS THE BASIS OF ROMESCO DE PEIX, THE CELEBRATED CATALAN SEAFOOD STEW.

raw large prawns (shrimp)	30
olive oil	1 tablespoon

romesco sauce

garlic	4 cloves, unpeeled
Roma (plum) tomato	1, halved and seeded
long red chillies	2
blanched almonds	2 tablespoons
hazelnuts	2 tablespoons
crusty white bread	2 thin slices
olive oil	for cooking
sun-dried capsicums (peppers) in oil, such as romesco or ancho	60 g (2¼ oz)
olive oil	1 tablespoon
red wine vinegar	1 tablespoon

Peel the prawns, leaving the tails intact. Cut down the back and gently pull out the dark vein, starting at the head end. Mix the prawns with ¼ teaspoon salt and refrigerate for 30 minutes.

To make the romesco sauce, preheat the oven to 200°C (400°F/Gas 6). Wrap the garlic cloves in foil, put on a baking tray with the tomato and chillies and bake for about 12 minutes. Spread the almonds and hazelnuts on the tray and bake for another 3–5 minutes. Leave to cool for 15 minutes. Fry the bread in a little olive oil, then break into rough pieces.

Transfer the almonds, hazelnuts and fried bread pieces to a small blender or food processor and blend until finely ground. Pop the garlic out of its skin and add to the blender. Next, add the seeded tomato to the blender. Split the chillies and remove the seeds. Scrape the flesh into the blender, discarding the skins. Pat the capsicums dry with paper towels, then chop them and add to the blender with the olive oil, vinegar, some salt and 2 tablespoons water. Blend until smooth, adding more water if necessary to form a soft dipping consistency. Leave for 30 minutes.

Heat the olive oil in a frying pan over high heat and cook the prawns for 5 minutes, or until curled up and slightly pink. Serve with the romesco sauce.

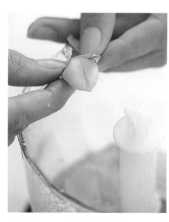

Add the garlic flesh to the ground nuts and bread in the blender.

Add the remaining ingredients and blend until smooth.

calamares
a la plancha . . . . serves 6

'A LA PLANCHA' MEANS COOKING ON A HOT FLAT PLATE, AS OPPOSED TO 'A LA PARILLA', WHICH MEANS ON THE GRILL. A LA PLANCHA IS A FAVOURITE METHOD IN MANY TAPAS BARS, AND CALAMARI PREPARED THIS WAY — SWEET AND TENDER, SLIGHTLY CHARRED AND SPRINKLED WITH PARSLEY AND GARLIC — ARE ESPECIALLY GOOD.

small squid	500 g (1 lb 2 oz)
olive oil	2 tablespoons

parsley dressing

extra virgin olive oil	2 tablespoons
flat-leaf (Italian) parsley	2 tablespoons finely chopped
garlic	1 clove, crushed

To clean the squid, gently pull the tentacles away from the hood (the intestines should come away at the same time). Remove the intestines from the tentacles by cutting under the eyes, then remove the beak if it remains in the centre of the tentacles by using your fingers to push up the centre. Discard the beak. Pull away the soft bone from the hood.

Rub the hoods under cold running water. The skin should come away easily. Wash the hoods and tentacles and drain well. Transfer to a bowl, add ¼ teaspoon salt and mix well. Cover and refrigerate for 30 minutes.

Just before cooking, whisk the dressing ingredients with some salt and ¼ teaspoon freshly ground black pepper in a jug or bowl.

Heat the oil in a frying pan over high heat and cook the squid hoods in small batches for 2–3 minutes, or until the hoods turn white and are tender. Cook the squid tentacles, turning to brown them all over, for 1 minute, or until they curl up. Serve hot, drizzled with the parsley dressing.

To prepare the squid, first pull the tentacles away from the hood.

Cut under the eyes and reserve the tentacles.

Grasp the soft bone in the hood and pull out. Discard.

Wash the squid hoods under running water, removing the skin.

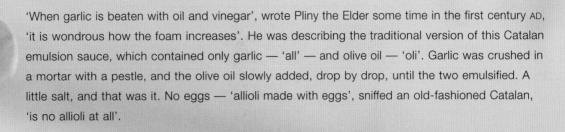

allioli

'When garlic is beaten with oil and vinegar', wrote Pliny the Elder some time in the first century AD, 'it is wondrous how the foam increases'. He was describing the traditional version of this Catalan emulsion sauce, which contained only garlic — 'all' — and olive oil — 'oli'. Garlic was crushed in a mortar with a pestle, and the olive oil slowly added, drop by drop, until the two emulsified. A little salt, and that was it. No eggs — 'allioli made with eggs', sniffed an old-fashioned Catalan, 'is no allioli at all'.

Be that as it may, today, because it's easier (and because the original allioli is almost unbearably garlicky), it is made with eggs. We can breathe easy.

But not too easy. Allioli should be strongly garlic in flavour, and smooth and white in texture. It is the ideal sauce for seafood of all types, and is perfect with potatoes and even (with honey stirred through it) quince. There is another version known as drowned allioli, a kind of curdled sauce, which is stirred into fish soups and stews. Whatever kind of allioli you are making, be sure that all ingredients are at room temperature before you start. For best results use a mild, late-season extra virgin olive oil.

Put ½ teaspoon sea salt and 4–6 garlic cloves in a mortar and gently mash to a paste with the pestle. Transfer to a food processor and add 2 egg yolks and 2 teaspoons white wine vinegar (optional). Process for several seconds. Now, using 250 ml (9 fl oz/1 cup) mild extra virgin olive oil and with the motor running, start adding the oil, drop by drop. When the mixture starts coming together, add the oil in a slow steady stream, until you have a thick mayonnaise. If at some point the mayonnaise becomes too thick, add a dash of vinegar and continue adding the oil.

tortilla

SUCH A SIMPLE DISH, SO DIFFICULT TO PERFECT. A TORTILLA MUST BE LIGHT, THE POTATO FIRM, THE ONIONS EVER SO SLIGHTLY CARAMELIZED, AND THE EGGS COOKED ENOUGH TO HOLD THE WHOLE THING TOGETHER BUT NO MORE. THE TORTILLA IS THE DISH BY WHICH A TAPAS BAR IS JUDGED.

potatoes	500 g (1 lb 2 oz), peeled and cut into 1 cm (1/2 inch) slices
olive oil	60 ml (2 fl oz/1/4 cup)
brown onion	1, thinly sliced
garlic	4 cloves, thinly sliced
flat-leaf (Italian) parsley	2 tablespoons finely chopped
eggs	6

Put the potato slices in a large saucepan, cover with cold water and bring to the boil over high heat. Boil for 5 minutes, then drain and set aside.

Put the oil in a deep-sided non-stick frying pan and heat over medium heat. Add the onion and garlic and cook for 5 minutes, or until the onion softens.

Add the potato and parsley to the pan and stir to combine. Cook over medium heat for 5 minutes, gently pressing on the mixture.

Whisk the eggs with 1 teaspoon each of salt and freshly ground black pepper and pour evenly over the potato. Cover and cook over low–medium heat for 20 minutes, or until the eggs are just set. Slide onto a serving plate or serve directly from the pan.

Aficionados of Spanish cooking rightly judge the tortilla to be one of the great exemplars of Spain's culinary tradition of 'direct and simple' cooking. Indeed it is, as well as being the subject of folk tales and a topic for argument in bars and kitchens across Spain. Nobody disagrees that its main ingredients are eggs and potatoes, but will fight almost to the death over the inclusion or not of garlic and onions. However, all agree that it should go no further. There are other 'tortillas' — a delicious one from Andalusia, called tortilla de berenjenas, which features eggplant (aubergine) — but if the recipe or menu just says tortilla, expect no more than potato — and perhaps garlic and onion.

scrambled eggs
with asparagus..serves 4

CREAMY SCRAMBLED EGGS AS A STARTER? WHY NOT. THAT'S WHAT THE SPANISH CALL A REVUELTO: EGGS WITH
FRESH SEASONAL INGREDIENTS LIKE GARLIC SHOOTS, BABY ARTICHOKES — AND ASPARAGUS.

garlic	2 cloves, chopped
bread	1 thick slice, crusts removed
olive oil	60 ml (2 fl oz/1/4 cup)
asparagus	175 g (6 oz/1 bunch), cut into 2 cm (3/4 inch) lengths
sweet pimentón (paprika)	1 teaspoon
white wine vinegar	2 tablespoons
eggs	6

Put the garlic and bread in a food processor or mortar and grind or pound to a loose paste, adding a small amount of water (about 1–2 tablespoons).

Heat the oil in a frying pan and sauté the asparagus over medium heat for 2 minutes, or until just starting to become tender. Add the garlic paste, pimentón, vinegar and a pinch of salt and stir to combine. Cover and cook over medium heat for 2–3 minutes, or until the asparagus is tender.

Beat the eggs and add to the pan. Reduce the heat to low and gently fold the eggs through with a whisk or wooden fork. Remove the eggs from the heat just before they are fully cooked, then season to taste and serve immediately.

Revuelto comes from the verb revolver, meaning to disturb, mess up, move about or turn over, all of which you do, gently and quickly, to make this delicious dish. The classic revuelto is made with the heads of esparragos trigueros, the tiny wild asparagus that covers the countryside in spring, or with asparagus combined with gambas (prawns). In expensive restaurants, you will even find a revuelto of truffles in season. The trick, when making this dish, is to not overcook it, but to move the eggs constantly with a whisk or a wooden fork. Also, remove the eggs from the heat just before they are cooked — they'll continue to cook in the pan — and serve them soft and just set.

the coastline

Spain's long coastline stretches from France to Africa, and is lapped by the Mediterranean Sea, the Atlantic Ocean and the Cantabrian Sea. This geography and a history of invasions and occupations by Phoenicians, Greeks, Romans, Moors, Jews and, last but not least, tourists, explains the wonderful variety of dishes to be found on the coast and on the Balearic Islands.

For many, Galicia, in the country's northwestern corner, is the seafood capital of Spain. Here you'll find culinary curiosities such as percebes (goose barnacles). These delicious morsels, eaten raw or lightly boiled, look like tiny elephant's feet and are plucked from wave-lashed rocks by intrepid gatherers. Daily, fishing boats deliver to the markets fresh langostas and bogavantes (spiny lobsters and lobsters) and buey, the large crab named after the ox. All three are boiled in seawater by Galician cooks and served simply as a mariscada (seafood platter).

Similar seafood, similarly treated, is to be found all along the Cantabrian coast, but special mention must be made of the delicious anchoas (anchovies) of the Basque country, which are usually washed down with chacoli, the crisp white wine of Guetaria, grown on the slopes overlooking the sea from which the fish have come.

In winter, all along the Spanish Atlantic coast, in estuaries and the mouths of rivers, wherever eels spawn, angulas (baby eels) are caught. This expensive luxury is usually fried with garlic and dried capsicums (peppers), a dish known as angulas a la bilbaina (Bilbao-style baby eels). But if we move into Catalonia and the Mediterranean, we'll find an altogether different kettle of fish on offer. Here, besides the elaborate Catalan seafood stew zarzuela, Catalans love calamares a la plancha (grilled calamari), salmonetes al horno (baked red mullet) or una parillada de mariscos (mixed grill of fish and/or shellfish).

Finally, in the southernmost province of Andalusia, you will find exquisitely fried fish being eaten in freidurías (shops specializing in frying). Andalusian frying is famed and the secret to their technique lies in large quantities of hot olive oil. Try filetes de merluza (hake steaks), acedías (wedge sole), fans of anchovies tied by the tail or cazón (dogfish) marinated in vinegar, garlic and cumin, then fried.

Besides seafood, the other great coastal ingredient is rice. First introduced by the Moors, rice has been cultivated continually in coastal wetlands and river valleys, and is used in hundreds of dishes around the coast, the most famous of which is paella, which has become, without question, Spain's national dish.

pulpo gallego . . . . serves 4

MELT-IN-THE-MOUTH OCTOPUS, RED WITH PIMENTÓN AND GLISTENING WITH EXTRA VIRGIN OLIVE OIL, MAKES PULPO GALLEGO A LONG-STANDING FAVOURITE IN TAPAS BARS. IT IS USUALLY SERVED ON A WOODEN PLATTER, FRESH OFF THE GRILL. FOR COMPLETE ENJOYMENT, SERVE WITH A GALICIAN RIBEIRO OR SIMILAR YOUNG WINE.

octopus	2, weighing approximately 500 g (1 lb 2 oz) each
bay leaf	1
black peppercorns	10
smoked or sweet pimentón (paprika)	for sprinkling
extra virgin olive oil	2 tablespoons
lemon wedges	to serve

Wash the octopus. Using a sharp knife, carefully cut between the head and tentacles of the octopus, just below the eyes. Grasp the body of the octopus and push the beak up and out through the centre of the tentacles with your fingers. Discard. Cut the eyes from the head of the octopus by slicing the small disc off with a sharp knife. Discard the eye section.

To clean the octopus head, carefully slit through one side (taking care not to break the ink sac) and scrape out any gut from inside. Rinse under running water to remove any remaining gut.

Bring a large saucepan of water to the boil. Add the bay leaf, peppercorns, 1 teaspoon salt and the octopus pieces. Reduce the heat and simmer for 1 hour, or until tender.

Remove the octopus from the water, drain well and leave for about 10 minutes.

Cut the tentacles into 1 cm (1/2 inch) thick slices and cut the head into bite-sized pieces. Arrange on a serving platter and sprinkle with pimentón and salt. Drizzle with the extra virgin olive oil and garnish with lemon wedges.

To prepare the octopus, first cut the head from the tentacles.

Remove the beak by pushing it up and out through the tentacles.

Cut the small disc — the eye — away from the head and discard.

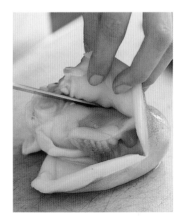

Carefully scrape away the gut from the head and discard.

bacalao with red capsicum .... serves 6

CERTAIN COMBINATIONS OF INGREDIENTS JUST NATURALLY WORK WELL. ONE SUCH COMBINATION IS THAT OF BACALAO (SALT COD) WITH SWEET RED CAPSICUM (PEPPER) AND TOMATOES, AS THIS DISH HAPPILY PROVES. IT IS FOUND, IN VARIOUS FORMS, ON TABLES RIGHT THROUGHOUT SPAIN.

bacalao (salt cod)	400 g (14 oz)
red capsicum (pepper)	1
olive oil	1 tablespoon
onion	1 small, chopped
garlic	1 clove, crushed
chilli flakes	1/4 teaspoon
sweet pimentón (paprika)	1 teaspoon
dry white wine	60 ml (2 fl oz/1/4 cup)
vine-ripened tomatoes	2, finely chopped
tomato paste (purée)	1 tablespoon
flat-leaf (Italian) parsley	1 tablespoon chopped

Soak the bacalao in plenty of cold water for 20 hours, changing the water four or five times to remove excess saltiness. Add the bacalao to a saucepan of boiling water, reduce the heat — it should be no more than 65°C (150°F) — and gently poach for 35–45 minutes. Drain and leave until cool. Remove the skin and flake the fish into large pieces, removing any bones. Put in a bowl.

Preheat the grill (broiler). Cut the capsicum into quarters, remove the seeds and grill (broil), skin side up, until the skin blackens and blisters. Cool in a plastic bag, then peel. Slice thinly.

Heat the oil in a saucepan over medium heat, add the onion and cook, stirring occasionally, for 3 minutes, or until translucent. Add the garlic, chilli and pimentón and cook for 1 minute. Increase the heat to high, add the white wine and simmer for 30 seconds. Reduce the heat, add the tomato and tomato paste and cook, stirring occasionally, for 5 minutes, or until thick. Add the bacalao, cover and simmer for about 5 minutes. Add the capsicum and parsley and taste before seasoning with salt. Serve hot.

There are almost as many Basque recipes for bacalao as there used to be cod in the waters of the North Atlantic. The most famous of these recipes is bacalao pil pil, which is, quite simply, salt cod in a rich and creamy emulsion of olive oil and garlic. This dish here, an example of the many that team salt cod with red capsicum (pepper) and tomatoes, works wonders by balancing the sweetness of the capsicum and the acidity of the tomatoes with the texture and slight residual saltiness of the fish. Bacalao also works well with pimentón, garlic, onion and eggplant (aubergine). This dish is a variation on the many which probably originated in the Vizcaya region, whose capital is Bilbao.

bacalao

Over one thousand years ago, Basque fishermen regularly set off from the coast of northern Spain for Newfoundland, off the eastern coast of Canada, a distance of some 4500 kilometres (2800 miles). Their original quarry was the whale, whale meat being a delicacy in medieval times. But soon they became aware of a fishery so vast that it was said you could step off a boat and walk across the water on the backs of the fish swarming in the icy waters. The fish were Atlantic cod (*Gadus morhua*).

The cod were transported to the markets of Europe just as whale meat was — salted and dried where it was caught. The result, bacalao, became a staple of the Spanish and Portuguese table for Lent, an answer to devout Catholic prayers for an economical fish for the Friday abstention meal. However, in 1992, after a millennium of exploitation, the vast fisheries off Newfoundland collapsed, and have yet to recover. Bacalao, now from Norway, is no longer a cheap staple, but a luxury for connoisseurs.

Why eat bacalao when fresh fish is so available? Why eat ham when you can eat pork? It is a separate product, much loved for its unique flavour and texture, and for the dishes that have evolved around it.

Cooking bacalao is not a straightforward process. First, you must choose a well-cured piece (avoid the cheaper but inferior product made from ling fish). Good bacalao has white, flexible meat, dark skin and a unique smell; the best cuts tend to appear around Easter. But before you cook your bacalao, you must prepare it. There are two ways to do this. One is to grill it over coals until it goes soft and damp. It is then easy to remove the bones and skin, and to rinse the flesh in water to remove excess salt. The second way, the time-honoured method, is to submerge the fish in fresh water for 20 hours, changing the water four or five times, then to poach it in water no hotter than 65°C (150°F) for 35–45 minutes. This is also a good test of the quality of your bacalao. If it is of poor quality, it will collapse into a fibrous mass. If it is of good quality, it will emerge smooth, firm and white — and without the oversalted flavour of badly cooked bacalao dishes.

sardinas murcianas..serves 6

ALL ALONG THE MURCIAN COAST, IN SPAIN'S SOUTHEAST, SARDINES ARE LANDED AND TRANSPORTED, STILL FLAPPING, TO KITCHENS ALONG THE SEAFRONT. WITH SEAFOOD, FRESHNESS IS ALL, BUT THIS IS ESPECIALLY SO FOR SPAIN'S MUCH-LOVED SARDINA.

vine-ripened tomatoes	1 kg (2 lb 4 oz)
fresh large sardines	24, cleaned, with backbones, heads and tails removed
green capsicums (peppers)	2, seeded and cut into thin rings
onion	1, sliced into thin rings
potatoes	2, cut into 5 mm (1/4 inch) thick slices
flat-leaf (Italian) parsley	2 tablespoons chopped, plus extra, to garnish
garlic	3 cloves, crushed
saffron threads	1/4 teaspoon, lightly roasted
olive oil	2 tablespoons

Score a cross in the base of each tomato. Put in a bowl of boiling water for 10 seconds, then plunge into cold water and peel away the skin from the cross. Cut each tomato into thin slices.

Preheat the oven to 180°C (350°F/Gas 4). Lightly oil a large, shallow earthenware or ceramic baking dish wide enough to hold the sardines. On a wooden board or clean work surface, gently open out the sardines and lightly sprinkle the insides with salt. Fold them back into their original shape.

Cover the base of the baking dish with a third of the tomato. Layer half the sardines on top. Follow with a layer of half the capsicum, then half the onion, then half the potatoes. Sprinkle with half the parsley and garlic, and season with freshly ground black pepper. Crumble half the saffron over the top.

Layer the remaining sardines, half the remaining tomatoes and then the other ingredients as before. Finish with the last of the tomatoes. Season well with salt and freshly ground black pepper. Drizzle the olive oil over the surface and cover with foil. Bake for 1 hour, or until the potatoes are cooked. Spoon off any excess liquid, sprinkle with extra parsley and serve straight from the dish.

Gently open the sardines out and sprinkle with salt.

Fill a dish with alternate layers of filling and sardine, then cook.

octopus in
garlic almond sauce ....serves 4

THIS IS A MODERN RECIPE, COMBINING CLASSIC INGREDIENTS FROM THE OLD WORLD — OCTOPUS, GARLIC AND
ALMONDS — WITH A CLASSIC INGREDIENT FROM THE NEW — RED CAPSICUM (PEPPER). THE RESULT: A MARRIAGE
OF WONDERFUL FLAVOUR AND TEXTURE.

baby octopus	1 kg (2 lb 4 oz)
red capsicum (pepper)	1/2 small, seeded
flaked almonds	125 g (41/2 oz)
garlic	3 cloves, crushed
red wine vinegar	80 ml (21/2 fl oz/1/3 cup)
olive oil	185 ml (6 fl oz/3/4 cup)
flat-leaf (Italian) parsley	2 tablespoons chopped

Using a small knife, carefully cut between the head and tentacles
of the octopus and use your fingers to push the beak up and out
through the centre of the tentacles. Discard. To clean the octopus
head, carefully slit through one side and pull out or chop out the
gut. Rinse under running water. Drop the octopus into a large
saucepan of boiling water and simmer for 20–40 minutes,
depending on their size, or until tender. After 15 minutes cooking,
start pricking the octopus with a skewer to test for tenderness.
When ready, remove the pan from the heat and cool the octopus
in the water for 15 minutes.

To make the sauce, heat the grill (broiler) to high. Grill (broil) the
capsicum skin side up until the skin blackens and blisters all over.
Cool in a plastic bag. Peel away the skin, put in a food processor
with the almonds and garlic, and purée. With the motor running,
gradually add the vinegar followed by the oil. Stir in 125 ml (4 fl oz/
1/2 cup) boiling water and the parsley, and season to taste with
salt and freshly ground black pepper.

To serve, cut the tentacles into pieces. Put all the octopus pieces
in a serving bowl with the sauce and toss to coat. Serve warm,
or chill and serve as a light salad.

First cut the head away from the
tentacles, then remove the beak.

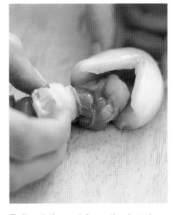
Pull out the gut from the head
and wash the head.

Remove the eye by simply slicing
away the small disc on the head.

three ways with seafood and wine

THE GRAPES GROWN AND HARVESTED ALONG SPANISH COASTLINES AND RIVER BANKS OFTEN RETURN, AS WINE, TO BE UNITED WITH THE SEAFOOD PLUCKED FROM THAT SAME COAST OR RIVER, EITHER IN THE PREPARATION OF DISHES OR AS AN ACCOMPANIMENT TO THEIR EATING. A CHILLED ROSADO (ROSÉ) WITH CALAMARES A LA PLANCHA AT A BEACHSIDE RESTAURANT, A SPLASH OF WHITE WINE INTO A PAN OF SAUTÉED MUSSELS, OR A DASH OF FINO SHERRY INTO THE COOKING POT CONTAINING FRESH CLAMS ARE JUST A FEW WAYS THE TWO CAN BE UNITED.

scallops with cava sauce

Remove and discard the vein, membrane or hard white muscle from 20 large white scallops. Remove the roe. Melt 60 g (2¼ oz) butter in a large heavy-based frying pan over medium–high heat. Sauté the scallops for 1–2 minutes on each side, or until almost cooked through. Transfer to a plate. Add 2 tablespoons thinly sliced French shallots to the pan and cook for 3 minutes, or until soft. Add 375 ml (13 fl oz/1½ cups) cava or other sparkling wine and simmer for 6–8 minutes, or until reduced by half. Stir in 250 ml (9 fl oz/1 cup) cream and simmer for about 10 minutes, or until the liquid is reduced to a sauce consistency. Stir in 2–3 teaspoons lemon juice and season. Return the scallops to the sauce to reheat gently, then serve garnished with 1 tablespoon chopped flat-leaf (Italian) parsley. Serves 4.

clams in fino sherry

Soak 1 kg (2 lb 4 oz) clams in salted water for 1 hour to release any grit. Rinse under running water and discard any open clams. Heat 2 tablespoons extra virgin olive oil in a heavy saucepan, then add 2 finely chopped garlic cloves and fry until lightly golden. Add 125 ml (4 fl oz/½ cup) fino sherry, 2 tablespoons chopped flat-leaf (Italian) parsley and season lightly. Add the clams and cook, covered, for about 4 minutes, shaking the pan vigorously a few times. Discard any clams that do not open. Serve the rest, with the sauce, hot or cold. Serves 4.

sherry with oysters

Not so much a recipe as a revelation. First, shuck your live oysters using a sharp purpose-made oyster knife. To do this, wrap a tea towel around your hand and use that hand to hold the first oyster, rounded side down. Insert the knife between the two shells, near the hinge. Twist the knife to separate the shells; this will sever the muscle that connects the oyster to the shell. Slide the knife blade underneath the oyster to detach it from the shell. Repeat with the remaining oysters (if unsure, ask your fishmonger for a lesson). Put the oysters on a bed of ice and eat, with no accompaniments (a squeeze of lemon juice if you must) except a glass of chilled fino or manzanilla sherry. This marriage of freshly shucked oysters and chilled dry sherry is a nigh on perfect match of texture, flavour and weight. Allow 4–6 oysters per person.

scallops with cava sauce

clams with white wine .... serves 4

WHAT COULD BE SIMPLER AND MORE DELICIOUS THAN FRESH CLAMS STEAMED OPEN IN WHITE WINE AND GARLIC,
THE FLAVOURS MINGLING WITH THE CLAM'S OWN JUICES OF THE SEA.

clams	1 kg (2 lb 4 oz)
vine-ripened tomatoes	2 large
olive oil	2 tablespoons
onion	1 small, finely chopped
garlic	2 cloves, crushed
flat-leaf (Italian) parsley	1 tablespoon chopped
nutmeg	a pinch
dry white wine	80 ml (2¹/₂ fl oz/¹/₃ cup)

Soak the clams in salted water for 1 hour to release any grit. Rinse under running water and discard any open clams.

Score a cross in the base of each tomato. Place in a bowl of boiling water for 10 seconds, then plunge into cold water and peel away the skin from the cross. Cut the tomatoes in half and scoop out the seeds with a teaspoon. Finely chop the tomatoes.

Heat the oil in a large flameproof casserole dish and cook the onion over low heat for 5 minutes, or until softened. Add the garlic and tomato and cook for 5 minutes. Add the parsley and nutmeg and season with salt and pepper. Add 80 ml (2¹/₂ fl oz/¹/₃ cup) water.

Add the clams and cook, covered, over low heat until they open (discard any that do not open). Add the wine and cook over low heat for 3–4 minutes, or until the sauce thickens, gently moving the casserole dish back and forth a few times, rather than stirring, so that the clams stay in the shells. Serve immediately, with bread.

The surrounding seas deliver a variety of clams onto Spanish tables, most often the almeja (carpet shell), but also the coquina (wedge shell), berberecho (cockle) and the curious-looking navaja (razor clam), which does indeed resemble an old-fashioned razor blade. Clams are treated simply in Spanish cooking: they are steamed open and eaten; thrown on a chargrill pan; or tossed into a simple steaming broth, such as here, and flavoured with ingredients like wine, garlic and tomatoes. On the Catalan coast, where pasta is common, the little town of Gandía makes a dish that combines clams with the short thin pasta, fideus.

rice with stuffed squid

.... serves 4

THIS IS ANOTHER EXAMPLE OF THE GLORIOUS RICE DISHES TO BE FOUND IN SPAIN. HERE, SHORT-GRAINED RICE IS TEAMED WITH SWEET, PLUMP LITTLE SQUID STUFFED WITH CURRANTS AND PINE NUTS.

small squid	8
onion	1 small
olive oil	2 tablespoons
currants	2 tablespoons
pine nuts	2 tablespoons
fresh breadcrumbs	25 g (1 oz/1/3 cup)
mint	1 tablespoon chopped
flat-leaf (Italian) parsley	1 tablespoon chopped
egg	1, lightly beaten
plain (all-purpose) flour	2 teaspoons

sauce

olive oil	1 tablespoon
onion	1 small, finely chopped
garlic	1 clove, crushed
dry white wine	60 ml (2 fl oz/1/4 cup)
chopped tomatoes	400 g (14 oz) can
sugar	1/2 teaspoon
bay leaf	1

rice

fish stock	1.25 litres (44 fl oz/5 cups)
olive oil	60 ml (2 fl oz/1/4 cup)
onion	1, finely chopped
garlic	3 cloves, crushed
short-grain rice	275 g (9 3/4 oz/1 1/4 cups)
cayenne pepper	1/4 teaspoon
squid ink	3 teaspoons (saved from the squid above or bought separately)
dry white wine	60 ml (2 fl oz/1/4 cup)
tomato paste (purée)	60 g (2 1/4 oz/1/4 cup)
flat-leaf (Italian) parsley	2 tablespoons chopped

To clean the squid, gently pull the tentacles away from the hood (the intestines should come away at the same time). Reserve the ink sac, if using in this recipe. Remove the intestines from the tentacles by cutting under the eyes, then remove the beak if it remains in the centre of the tentacles by using your fingers to push up the centre. Discard the beak. Pull away the soft bone from the hood.

Rub the hoods under cold running water. The skin should come away easily. Wash the hoods and tentacles and drain well.

Put the tentacles and onion in a processor and finely chop. Heat the oil in a saucepan and cook the currants and pine nuts over low heat until lightly browned. Remove from the pan. Add the onion mixture, cook gently for 5 minutes, then add to the pine nut mixture with the breadcrumbs, herbs and egg. Season. Stuff into the squid hoods, close the openings and secure with toothpicks. Dust with flour.

To make the sauce, heat the oil in a frying pan and cook the onion over low heat for 5 minutes, or until soft. Stir in the garlic, wine and 125 ml (4 fl oz/1/2 cup) water. Cook over high heat for 1 minute, then add the tomato, sugar and bay leaf. Season, reduce the heat and simmer for 5 minutes. Add the squid to the pan in a single layer. Simmer, covered, for 20 minutes, or until tender.

To make the rice, bring the stock to a simmer in a saucepan. Heat the oil in a saucepan and cook the onion over low heat until soft. Add the garlic, rice and cayenne pepper. Mix the squid ink with 4 tablespoons of the stock, add to the rice with the wine and tomato paste and stir until the liquid has almost evaporated. Add 250 ml (9 fl oz/1 cup) stock, simmer until this evaporates, then add the remaining stock, 250 ml (9 fl oz/1 cup) at a time, until the rice is tender and creamy. Cover and leave off the heat for about 5 minutes. Season and stir in the parsley. Put the rice on a serving plate, arrange the squid on top and spoon over the sauce.

three ways with tuna

THREE THOUSAND WAYS WITH TUNA WOULD BE JUST AS FEASIBLE FOR THIS FIRM-FLESHED AND FULL-BODIED FISH. TUNA HAS BEEN ENJOYED AND EATEN ALL AROUND THE MEDITERRANEAN SINCE TIME IMMEMORIAL. FRESH TUNA, EITHER ATÚN (BLUE FIN), ALBACORA (ALBACORE), BACORETA (LITTLE TUNNY) OR LISTADO (SKIPJACK), IS OFTEN SIMPLY BARBECUED OR CHARGRILLED, SPRINKLED WITH LEMON JUICE AND TOPPED WITH PARSLEY AND FRIED GARLIC CHIPS. YOU WILL ALSO SEE CANNED TUNA IN OLIVE OIL SERVED ON BOCADILLOS (BREAD ROLLS).

marmitako

Preheat the oven to 180°C (350°F/Gas 4). Heat 2 tablespoons olive oil in a saucepan over medium heat and add 1 diced onion, 1 seeded and roughly diced red capsicum (pepper) and 2 teaspoons sweet pimentón (paprika). Cook for 3 minutes, or until soft. Add another tablespoon oil if necessary, then add 2 finely chopped garlic cloves, 2 bay leaves and 250 g (9 oz/1 cup) canned chopped tomatoes and cook for 10 minutes. Add 80 ml (2½ fl oz/⅓ cup) white wine and 30 g (1 oz/¼ cup) drained capers and stir through. Peel 650 g (1 lb 7 oz) all-purpose potatoes and cut into 1 cm (½ inch) thick slices. Arrange the potato slices in the bottom of a shallow 26 x 20 cm (10½ x 8 inch) casserole or heatproof dish. Evenly spread the tomato and onion mixture over the potatoes and pour over 250 ml (9 fl oz/1 cup) chicken stock. Bake for 40 minutes, or until the potato is almost cooked. Season 4 x 200 g (7 oz) tuna steaks with salt and freshly ground black pepper and arrange on top of the potato. Bake for 5–8 minutes for rare or 10–15 minutes for medium. Season well and sprinkle 1 chopped handful flat-leaf (Italian) parsley, 1 tablespoon lemon juice and 1 seeded and finely chopped small red chilli (optional) over the top before serving. Serves 4.

atún con tomate

Combine 4 x 200 g (7 oz) tuna steaks with 80 ml (2½ fl oz/⅓ cup) lemon juice, 1 tablespoon chopped flat-leaf (Italian) parsley and a large pinch of salt, and leave to marinate for 15 minutes. Preheat the oven to 180°C (350°F/Gas 4). Heat 80 ml (2½ fl oz/⅓ cup) oil in a saucepan over medium heat and cook 1 finely chopped onion and 2 chopped garlic cloves for 5 minutes, or until translucent. Add 400 g (14 oz) can tomatoes, 1 bay leaf, 1 teaspoon sugar, 1 teaspoon chopped thyme and 1 tablespoon chopped flat-leaf (Italian) parsley, and season to taste. Increase the heat to high and cook for 3 minutes, or until some of the liquid has reduced. Heat 100 ml (3½ fl oz) oil in a large frying pan over medium–high heat. Drain the tuna steaks and coat in plain (all-purpose) flour. Cook for about 3 minutes on each side, or until golden, then transfer to a large casserole dish. Cover with the tomato sauce and bake for 20 minutes, or until the tuna flakes easily. Serves 4.

braised tuna

Flour and salt a thick 500 g (1 lb 2 oz) piece of fresh tuna. Add 100 ml (3½ fl oz) extra virgin olive oil to a deep flameproof casserole dish and set over medium heat. When the oil is hot, add the tuna. Turn it several times until it is coloured all over. Add 1 sliced onion, 2 chopped tomatoes, 2 finely chopped garlic cloves, 1 bay leaf and 150 ml (5 fl oz) white wine. Reduce the heat to low, cover and leave for 30–50 minutes, or until the tuna is thoroughly cooked. Remove the tuna from the pan, allow to cool, then cut into slices. Pass the sauce through a fine strainer and return to the dish. Reheat, then pour over the tuna. Serve with a green salad. Serves 4.

marmitako

trout with jamón..serves 4

THE COLD MOUNTAIN RIVERS OF NAVARRA TEEM WITH TROUT, WHICH ARE CAUGHT FOR SPORT AND EATING. THIS RECIPE, OFTEN CALLED TRUCHA A LA NAVARRA, USES BACON FAT AS THE COOKING MEDIUM; OLIVE OIL BEING FORMERLY AN EXPENSIVE LUXURY FOR THE NAVARRA COOKS. SERVE THIS DISH WITH A ROSÉ FROM THE AREA.

river trout	4 x 200 g (7 oz), cleaned and deboned
mint	80 g (2³/4 oz/1 bunch), broken into sprigs
white wine	185 ml (6 fl oz/³/4 cup)
jamón or prosciutto	8 slices
bacon fat or olive oil	2 tablespoons
lemon juice	2 tablespoons
butter	2 tablespoons cold, chopped

Stuff each trout cavity with several sprigs of mint. Arrange in a dish in which they fit together snugly and drizzle with the wine. Cover and marinate in the refrigerator for at least 6 hours.

Preheat the oven to 180°C (350°F/Gas 4). Remove the fish from the marinade and pat dry, reserving the marinade. Remove the mint from each trout cavity and discard. Season the cavity. Roll up 2 pieces of jamón per fish and put in the cavity with some more mint sprigs.

Heat the bacon fat in a large frying pan over medium heat for 4 minutes, or until melted. Add the fish and fry for 3 minutes on each side, or until crisp. Transfer the fish to an ovenproof dish and bake for 10 minutes, or until the fish is no longer translucent and can be flaked easily with a fork.

Meanwhile, combine the reserved marinade and lemon juice in the frying pan and boil over high heat for about 5 minutes, or until the sauce reduces to a syrupy consistency. Gradually whisk in the butter until the sauce is slightly glazy. Serve the fish with the jamón and mint inside, drizzled with the sauce.

Fill the cavity of each trout with jamón and fresh mint.

Gently fry the filled trout, in batches if necessary, until crisp.

Add the butter to the sauce, whisking until it turns shiny.

baked bream with capsicum, chilli and potatoes .... serves 4 to 6

WHO SAID FISH CAN'T MAKE A HEARTY MEAL? YOU WILL OFTEN FIND SATISFYING DISHES LIKE THIS ONE MARRYING FISH (SUCH AS HAKE AND BACALAO) WITH POTATOES, ESPECIALLY IN COLD AND ARID NORTHERN SPAIN.

whole red bream, red snapper or porgy	1.25 kg (2 lb 12 oz), cleaned
lemon	1
olive oil	60 ml (2 fl oz/¼ cup)
potatoes	800 g (1 lb 12 oz), thinly sliced
garlic	3 cloves, thinly sliced
flat-leaf (Italian) parsley	3 tablespoons finely chopped
red onion	1 small, thinly sliced
dried chilli	1 small, seeded and finely chopped
red capsicum (pepper)	1, seeded and cut into thin rings
yellow capsicum (pepper)	1, seeded and cut into thin rings
bay leaves	2
thyme	3–4 sprigs
dry sherry	60 ml (2 fl oz/¼ cup)

Cut off and discard the fins from the fish and put it in a large non-metallic dish. Cut 2 thin slices from the middle of the lemon and reserve. Squeeze the juice from the rest of the lemon into the cavity of the fish. Add 2 tablespoons of the oil and refrigerate, covered, for 2 hours.

Preheat the oven to 190°C (375°F/Gas 5) and lightly oil a shallow earthenware baking dish large enough to hold the whole fish. Spread half the potato slices on the base and scatter over the garlic, parsley, onion, chilli and capsicum. Season with salt and freshly ground black pepper. Cover with the rest of the potato. Pour in 80 ml (2½ fl oz/⅓ cup) water and sprinkle the remaining olive oil over the top. Cover with foil and bake for 1 hour.

Increase the oven temperature to 220°C (425°F/Gas 7). Season the fish inside and out with salt and pepper and put the bay leaves and thyme inside the cavity. Make 3 or 4 diagonal slashes on each side. Cut the reserved lemon slices in half. Nestle the fish onto the potato and fit the lemon slices into the slashes on the top side of the fish, to resemble fins. Bake, uncovered, for about 30 minutes, or until the fish is cooked through and the potato is golden and crusty.

Pour the sherry over the fish and return to the oven for 3 minutes. Serve straight from the dish.

Lay the vegetables and spices in a dish, with the potato on top.

Add the fish to the dish, fitting the lemon slices into its flesh.

three ways with salt

SPANISH FOOD IS SALTY. SALT IS USED UNSPARINGLY IN ALL SORTS OF FOOD PREPARATION: FOR EXAMPLE, WHERE ITALIANS CURE PROSCIUTTO BY RUBBING A LEG OF PORK WITH SALT, THE SPANISH BURY THEIRS IN SALT. LIKEWISE IN COOKING: SALT IS NOT SPARED WHEN MAKING COCIDOS (STEWS), RICE DISHES OR SOUPS. NO CONVINCING EXPLANATIONS ARE OFFERED FOR THIS STRANGE ADDICTION. WE CAN ONLY CONJECTURE THAT IT IS DUE TO THE EXCELLENCE AND ABUNDANCE OF SPANISH SALT, ESPECIALLY THE MINERAL-RICH SEA SALTS.

fish baked in salt

Preheat the oven to 200°C (400°F/Gas 6). Rinse 1.8 kg (4 lb) scaled and cleaned whole fish (such as blue-eye, jewfish, sea bass, groper), and pat dry inside and out with paper towels. Slice 2 lemons and put the slices into the fish cavity, along with 4 thyme sprigs and 1 thinly sliced fennel bulb. Pack 1.5 kg (3 lb 5 oz) rock salt into a large baking dish and put the fish on top. Cover with the same amount of salt again, pressing down until the salt is packed firmly around the fish. Bake the fish for 30–40 minutes, or until a skewer inserted into the centre of the fish comes out hot. Carefully remove the salt from the top of the fish and move to one side of the dish. Carefully peel the skin away, ensuring that no salt remains on the flesh. Serve hot or cold with allioli (page 48) or your choice of accompaniment. Serves 4–6.

prawns boiled in sea water

If you have access to clean sea water, collect 3 litres (105 fl oz/12 cups) of it, allow to stand for 1 hour, then carefully pour the water into a large saucepan, leaving behind any sediment. Fill a second large saucepan with water and plenty of ice. Bring the sea water to a rolling boil and add 1 kg (2 lb 4 oz) unshelled green prawns (shrimp). Cook for 3 minutes, then scoop the prawns out and plunge them into the iced water for 1 minute. Scoop out and serve (shelled or unshelled), with allioli (page 48) on the side. (If you don't have access to clean sea water, cook the prawns in exactly the same way in water in which you have dissolved 35 g (1 1/4 oz/1/4 cup) sea salt.) Serves 4.

anchovies on toast

Salted anchovies in olive oil are one of the great Spanish export products. The following is a popular Spanish snack. You will need to allow 2 anchovies, 2 strips marinated capsicum (pepper) (page 31), 2 pitted black olives and 1 slice crusty bread per person. Using a toothpick, fix the anchovies, strips of capsicum and black olives to a slice of crusty bread, then submerge the bread in a saucepan of very hot olive oil. Remove when the bread is golden brown, drain on paper towels and serve.

escabeche .... serves 4

THIS ANCIENT AND CURIOUS METHOD OF PREPARING AND PRESERVING FISH IS ALSO A DELICIOUSLY SWEET, SOUR AND SPICY DISH. THIS RECIPE IS A MODERN VARIATION ON THE BASIC ESCABECHE, AS IT USES ORANGE JUICE AND ZEST, BORROWED FROM THE SOUTH AMERICAN SEVICHE, ITSELF AN ADAPTATION OF ESCABECHE.

plain (all-purpose) flour	for dusting
skinless fish fillets, such as red mullet, whiting, redfish, garfish	500 g (1 lb 2 oz)
extra virgin olive oil	100 ml (3¹/₂ fl oz)
red onion	1, thinly sliced
garlic	2 cloves, thinly sliced
thyme	2 sprigs
ground cumin	1 teaspoon
spring onions (scallions)	2 finely chopped
orange zest	¹/₂ teaspoon finely grated
orange juice	60 ml (2 fl oz/¹/₄ cup)
white wine	185 ml (6 fl oz/³/₄ cup)
white wine vinegar	185 ml (6 fl oz/³/₄ cup)
pitted green olives	60 g (2¹/₄ oz), roughly chopped
caster (superfine) sugar	¹/₂ teaspoon

Mix a little salt and freshly ground black pepper into the flour and lightly dust the fish with the flour. Heat 2 tablespoons of the oil in a frying pan over medium heat and add the fish in batches. Cook the fish on both sides until lightly browned and just cooked through (the fish should flake easily when tested with a fork). Remove the fish from the pan and put in a single, flat layer in a large, shallow non-metallic dish.

Heat the remaining oil in the same pan, add the onion and garlic and cook, stirring, over medium heat for 5 minutes, or until soft.

Add the thyme, cumin and spring onion and stir until fragrant. Add the orange zest, orange juice, wine, vinegar, olives and sugar and freshly ground black pepper, to taste. Bring to the boil and pour over the fish. Allow to cool in the liquid, then refrigerate overnight. Serve at room temperature.

Escabeche is both the name of the dish and a form of preserving fish. It involves frying then marinating fish, a method that has survived, almost intact, since Roman times. The Roman Apicius (circa 80 BC–AD 40), whose recipes survive in fragments, records a dish of fried fish sprinkled with hot vinegar. The word escabeche comes down to us from the Arabic language of Medieval times, and the technique was also embellished by the cooks of that period. Apart from the Latin American seviche, escabeche has also migrated to many European countries. Today, this method of imparting a sweet-sour flavour to food is used with meat, vegetables and poultry.

skate with sherry vinegar

THE MEDITERRANEAN IS ALIVE WITH LAZILY FLAPPING RAYS AND SKATES, FROM WHOSE WINGS THIS DELICACY IS HARVESTED. HERE, IT IS TEAMED WITH ANOTHER FAVOURITE SPANISH INGREDIENT, SHERRY VINEGAR.

sherry vinegar	100 ml (3½ fl oz)
olive oil	80 ml (2½ fl oz/⅓ cup)
garlic	6 cloves, crushed
dried red chilli	1 small, seeded and chopped
flat-leaf (Italian) parsley	2 tablespoons chopped
sweet pimentón (paprika)	1 teaspoon
saffron threads	¼ teaspoon
dried oregano	1 teaspoon
vegetable oil	80 ml (2½ fl oz/⅓ cup)
brown onion	1, chopped
leek	1, chopped
skate fillets	4 x 200 g (7 oz)
lemon wedges	to serve, optional

Put the vinegar in a saucepan over high heat and bring to the boil. Boil for 3 minutes, or until reduced by half. Leave to cool, then add the olive oil, half the garlic, the chopped chilli and some salt. Meanwhile, combine the parsley, paprika, saffron threads and oregano in a mortar (or food processor) and pound to a paste.

Heat 2 tablespoons of the vegetable oil in a frying pan over medium heat and cook the spice paste, onion, leek and remaining garlic for 5 minutes, or until the onion and leek are translucent. Remove from the frying pan and set aside.

Add the remaining oil to the pan, add the skate in batches and brown each side for 4–5 minutes, depending on the thickness of the fillets. Remove and cover with foil to keep warm. Return the onion and leek mixture to the frying pan and heat through.

Drizzle the dressing over the fish and spoon over the onion and leek mixture. Garnish with lemon wedges, if using.

The wing flaps from the ray and skate are a Mediterranean delicacy often avoided by English-speaking cooks. However, there is no reason not to try them. The long strands of flesh found on the wings are delicious, and well worth the effort of getting to know the fish. Like shark and dogfish, ray and skate have cartilage rather than bones. Do not be put off by a slight smell of ammonia to the flesh when you buy it — this indicates health (a complex matter of the body chemistry of non-bony fish) and will disappear during cooking. For the same reason, it's best not to eat ray or skate too fresh — a day or two of ageing improves the flesh.

three ways with fish sauces

HERE ARE THREE ANCIENT DISHES COMBINING SEAFOOD WITH SAUCE: A TWELFTH CENTURY CATALAN JURVERT OR JOLIVERT — THAT IS, GREEN SAUCE — MODERNIZED AS SALSA VERDE AND SERVED WITH THAT MOST SPANISH OF FISH, MERLUZA (HAKE); AN UPDATED VERSION OF A MOORISH DISH OF SALMON IN ORANGE SAUCE; AND A MODERN VERSION OF A TRADITIONAL ASTURIAN FISHERMEN'S RECIPE FOR BOGAVANTE (LOBSTER). ALL THREE ARE EASY TO COOK AND WONDERFUL TO EAT IN THE TWENTY-FIRST CENTURY.

hake in green sauce

Dust 4 x 200 g (7 oz) hake steaks (or use gem fish) with seasoned flour, shaking off any excess. Heat 80 ml (2½ fl oz/⅓ cup) olive oil in a large frying pan over medium heat and add 3 chopped garlic cloves and 2 seeded and chopped green chillies. Cook for 1 minute, or until the garlic just starts to colour. Remove the garlic and chilli with a slotted spoon. Increase the heat to high and cook the hake for about 1 minute on each side. Remove from the pan. Add 125 ml (4 fl oz/½ cup) white wine, 170 ml (5½ fl oz/⅔ cup) fish stock, 2 tablespoons chopped flat-leaf (Italian) parsley and the garlic and chilli mixture to the pan and simmer until the sauce has thickened to your liking. Lightly blanch 12 asparagus spears and cut into 4 cm (1½ inch) lengths. Add them, the fish, 60 g (2¼ oz/½ cup) cooked green peas and 1 chopped handful parsley to the pan and simmer until the fish is cooked through. Serve immediately. Serves 4.

andalusian salmon in orange sauce

Finely julienne the pith-free zest of 4 Valencia oranges (or, better still, if you can get them, use the bitter orange from Seville) and squeeze their juice. Set both aside. Put 60 ml (2 fl oz/¼ cup) extra virgin olive oil and 2 finely chopped onions in a large non-reactive saucepan over medium heat and fry for 10 minutes, stirring frequently. Cut a skinless piece of salmon fillet weighing 1.25 kg (2 lb 12 oz) into 8 strips, then lightly flour the strips. Add the fish to the pan and cook with the onions for about 5 minutes, shaking the pan. Add the reserved orange juice, 1 tablespoon white wine vinegar, 2 tablespoons sugar, 250 ml (9 fl oz/1 cup) fish stock and cook for about 8 minutes over medium heat. Add the reserved julienned zest and cook, uncovered, until the sauce is syrupy and the fish is tender. Season and serve. Serves 4.

lobster in pimentón sauce

Buy 1 live rock lobster or lobster weighing 1.5 kg (3 lb 5 oz) or 2 smaller crayfish and dispatch by putting into the freezer for about 2 hours, then plunge into boiling water. Cut the lobster or crayfish into claws and 2 cm (¾ inch) rounds, conserving the mustard (contents of the head) and juices, if you wish. If unsure, ask your fishmonger to do this for you or buy pre-prepared frozen lobster rounds with the shell on. Put 125 ml (4 fl oz/½ cup) olive oil in a large non-reactive saucepan. Add 2 finely chopped onions, 1 whole red chilli and 1 tablespoon sweet pimentón (paprika) and fry over medium heat for 3 minutes. Add 200 ml (7 fl oz) fino sherry and let the alcohol cook off, taking care not to burn the pimentón. Add the lobster or cray pieces or rounds, with the mustard and juices, if using, and cook, uncovered, for 10–15 minutes over low–medium heat, or until the flesh is cooked and opaque. Put 2 tablespoons cornflour (cornstarch) and 250 ml (9 fl oz/1 cup) water in a saucepan and mix over low heat until incorporated. Add this to the lobster and stir through. Season with salt to taste, leave for 5 minutes and serve. Serves 4.

hake in green sauce

suquet de peix . . . . serves 4 to 6

THIS DISH IS ONE OF THE MYRIAD OF FISH AND SEAFOOD STEWS — ALMOST SOUPS — THAT CAN BE FOUND IN
SPAIN'S CATALAN-SPEAKING REGION, WHICH INCLUDES THE BALEARIC ISLANDS AND VALENCIA. SUQUET, FROM THE
VERB SUQUEJAR, MEANING TO SEEP, IMPLIES THAT THE FLAVOURS OF THE FISH 'SEEP' INTO THE SAUCE.

olive oil	1 tablespoon
carrot	1, finely diced
onion	1, finely diced
leek	1, finely diced
garlic	3 cloves, chopped
small red chilli	1, seeded and finely chopped
celery	1 stalk, finely diced
potatoes	2 large, cut into 2 cm (3/4 inch) dice
firm white fish fillets	500 g (1 lb 2 oz), cut into 2 cm (3/4 inch) dice, reserving any bones and scraps
bay leaf	1
white wine	250 ml (9 fl oz/1 cup)
brandy	30 ml (1 fl oz)
diced tomatoes	400 g (14 oz) can, drained
tomato paste (purée)	60 g (2 1/4 oz/1/4 cup)
mussels	12, debearded and scrubbed
raw king prawns (shrimp)	8, peeled and tails removed
lemon juice	2 tablespoons
flat-leaf (Italian) parsley	2 tablespoons chopped

Heat the oil in a large saucepan over medium heat. Add the
carrot, onion, leek, garlic, chilli and celery and cook for 5 minutes,
or until the onion is translucent. Add the potato and 1.5 litres
(52 fl oz/6 cups) cold water. Bring to the boil, then reduce the heat
and simmer for 8 minutes, or until the potato is semi-cooked. Stir
in the fish bones and scraps and bay leaf and simmer for about
6–8 minutes, or until the potato is soft. Strain the liquid and
reserve. Remove the bones, scraps and bay leaf, and purée the
remaining potato and vegetable mixture with the reserved liquid.

In a separate saucepan, combine the wine, brandy, diced tomato
and tomato paste and bring to the boil. Add the mussels and
cook, covered, for 3 minutes, or until opened. Remove from the
pan, discarding any mussels that remain closed.

Stir the mussel liquid into the potato purée. Transfer to a large
saucepan and bring to the boil. Add the fish pieces and prawns,
reduce the heat and simmer for 8 minutes, or until all the seafood
is cooked.

Stir in the mussels and lemon juice and gently heat through.
Season well and garnish with the parsley. This dish is delicious
served with fried bread and allioli (page 48).

Prepare the mussels by scrubbing
them, then removing the beard.

Cook the mussels in the tomato
mixture until they open.

zarzuela de pescado . . . . serves 6 to 8

THIS CATALAN FISH SOUP IS NAMED AFTER A SYTLE OF LIGHT OPERA, WHICH GIVES SOME IDEA OF ITS VITALITY. IT INCORPORATES A VARIETY OF SEAFOOD, AND IS BUILT AROUND A PICADA, DESCRIBED AS THE 'CATALAN ROUX'. A BLEND OF GARLIC, NUTS AND BREAD, A PICADA IS USED TO GIVE FORM TO, OR HOLD TOGETHER, DISHES.

red mullet fillets	300 g (10½ oz)
firm white fish fillets	400 g (14 oz)
calamari	300 g (10½ oz), cleaned
fish stock	1.5 litres (52 fl oz/6 cups)
olive oil	80 ml (2½ fl oz/⅓ cup)
onion	1, chopped
garlic	6 cloves, chopped
small red chilli	1, chopped
sweet pimentón (paprika)	1 teaspoon
saffron threads	a pinch
white wine	150 ml (5 fl oz)
crushed tomatoes	400 g (14 oz) can
raw medium prawns (shrimp)	16, peeled and deveined, tails intact
brandy	2 tablespoons
black mussels	24, debearded and scrubbed
flat-leaf (Italian) parsley	1 tablespoon chopped, to garnish

picada

olive oil	2 tablespoons
day-old bread	2 slices, diced
garlic	2 cloves
blanched almonds	5, roasted
flat-leaf (Italian) parsley	2 tablespoons

Cut the fish and calamari into 4 cm (1½ inch) pieces. Pour the stock into a large saucepan, bring to the boil and heat for about 20 minutes, or until reduced by half.

To make the picada, heat the olive oil in a frying pan, add the bread and stir for 3 minutes, or until golden, adding the garlic for the last minute. Process the bread, garlic, almonds and parsley in a food processor. Add enough stock to make a smooth paste.

Heat 2 tablespoons of the oil in a large saucepan, add the onion, garlic, chilli and paprika, and cook, stirring, for 1 minute. Add the saffron, white wine, tomato and stock. Bring to the boil, then reduce the heat and leave to simmer.

Heat the remaining oil in another frying pan over medium heat and cook the fish and calamari for 3–5 minutes. Remove from the pan. Add the prawns, cook for 1 minute, then add the brandy. Carefully ignite the brandy and let the flames burn down. Remove the prawns from the pan.

Add the mussels to the hot stock and simmer, covered, for about 3 minutes, or until opened. Discard any that do not open. Return all the seafood to the saucepan, add the picada, and stir until the sauce has thickened slightly and the seafood is cooked. Season to taste. Serve garnished with parsley.

Cut the fish into cubes, then cut the calamari in the same way.

Process the picada ingredients to a paste, adding stock to thin it.

rice

There is a story from Valencia, the traditional home of paella, that dates from the War of Independence fought against France (1808–1814). So impressed was a French general with the paella cooked by a local woman that he promised that for each new rice dish she cooked, he would free a Spanish prisoner of war. He was removed from his post after she had cooked 176 dishes — and she hadn't finished yet.

This anecdote is a polite Spanish way of saying there is more to Spanish rice dishes than paella, which, you might be surprised to know, in its original incarnation as paella valenciana de la huerta (Valencian paella from the vegetable garden) does not contain fish or shellfish.

Paella originated in the fertile coastal strip of the Ebro River delta region near Valencia. Its ingredients included rabbit, chicken, tomato, saffron, local dried and green beans and always, after that, controversy. Rosemary? No! Yes! Peas? Yes! No! There will always be debate in Valencia about the true ingredients of a paella.

Today, of course, we make paella with seafood. And why not? A cuisine that doesn't adapt and change is likely to end up in a museum. But we should not forget the other remarkable rice dishes of Spain, including the classic Valencian dish arroz con judias blancas y nabos (rice with white beans and turnips), which many claim is the greatest rice dish of all; or arroz negro (rice blackened with squid ink), also from Valencia; or arroz al horno (baked rice with chickpeas and garlic) from the Balearic Islands.

To make this multitude of rice dishes, there is a range of short-grained rice varieties, two of the most famous being Calasparra from the Murcian Segura River valley, which has a Denominación de Origen (DO), and the highly absorbent and nutty-flavoured Bomba from Valencia, a variety originally planted by the Moors.

seafood paella . . . . serves 4

PAELLA IS THE DISH BY WHICH SPANISH FOOD IS DEFINED INTERNATIONALLY. IT ORIGINATED IN THE RICE-GROWING EBRO RIVER DELTA AREA, INLAND FROM THE CITY OF VALENCIA, BUT NOW FIRMLY BELONGS, WITH DELICIOUS SEAFOOD ADDED, TO THE WHOLE COUNTRY.

white wine	125 ml (4 fl oz/½ cup)
red onions	1½, finely chopped
black mussels	12–16, debearded and scrubbed
olive oil	125 ml (4 fl oz/½ cup)
bacon	1 rasher, finely chopped
garlic	4 cloves, crushed
red capsicum (pepper)	1, seeded and finely chopped
vine-ripened tomato	1, peeled and chopped
chorizo	90 g (3½ oz), thinly sliced
cayenne pepper	a pinch
paella or short-grain rice	225 g (8 oz/1 cup)
saffron threads	¼ teaspoon
chicken stock	500 ml (17 fl oz/2 cups), heated
fresh or frozen peas	85 g (3 oz/½ cup)
raw prawns (shrimp)	12, peeled and deveined, tails left intact
squid tubes	2, cleaned and cut into rings
white fish fillets	115 g (4 oz), skinned and cut into pieces
flat-leaf (Italian) parsley	2 tablespoons finely chopped

Heat the wine and two-thirds of the onion in a saucepan. Add the mussels, cover and gently shake the pan for 5 minutes over high heat. Remove from the heat, discard any mussels that did not open and drain, reserving the liquid. Heat the oil in a large heavy-based frying pan, add the remaining onion, bacon, garlic and capsicum, and cook for 5 minutes. Add the tomato, chorizo and cayenne pepper. Season. Stir in the reserved liquid, then add the rice and stir again.

Blend the saffron with the stock, then stir into the rice mixture. Bring to the boil, then reduce the heat to low and gently simmer, uncovered, for 15 minutes without stirring.

Put the peas, prawns, squid and fish on top of the rice. Push them in, cover and cook over low heat for 10 minutes, turning the seafood over halfway through cooking time, until the rice is tender and the seafood is cooked through. Add the mussels for the last 5 minutes to heat through. If the rice is not quite cooked, add extra stock and cook for a few more minutes. Allow to rest for 5 minutes, then sprinkle over the parsley and serve.

Prepare all the seafood first; peel and devein the prawns.

Add the rice to the paella, stirring to incorporate it.

txangurro . . . . serves 4

THE BASQUE WORD FOR CRAB IS THE NAME GIVEN TO THIS JUSTLY CELEBRATED DISH OF CRAB STUFFED WITH ITS OWN MEAT, WINE AND GARLIC. IT IS A DELICIOUS ILLUSTRATION OF THE BASQUE GENIUS FOR DEVISING SEAFOOD DISHES THAT COMPLEMENT THE FLAVOUR OF THE CENTRAL INGREDIENT — IN THIS CASE, THE CRAB.

live large-bodied crabs, such as centollo or spider	4, weighing about 750 g (1 lb 10 oz) each
olive oil	80 ml (2 1/2 fl oz/1/3 cup)
onion	1, finely chopped
garlic	1 clove
dry white wine	125 ml (4 fl oz/1/2 cup)
puréed tomato or tomato passata	250 g (9 oz/1 cup)
dry breadcrumbs	2 tablespoons
flat-leaf (Italian) parsley	2 tablespoons chopped
butter	40 g (1 1/2 oz), chopped into small pieces

To dispatch the crabs, put them in the freezer for 45 minutes, so they will lose consciousness. Bring a large saucepan of water to the boil. Stir in 3 tablespoons salt, then add the crabs. Return to the boil and simmer, uncovered, for 15 minutes. Remove the crabs from the water and allow to cool for 30 minutes. Extract the meat from the legs. Open the body without destroying the upper shell, which is needed for serving, reserving any liquid in a bowl. Take out the meat and put with the leg meat. Finely chop all the meat. Scoop out all the brown paste from the shells and mix with the chopped meat.

Heat the olive oil in a frying pan and cook the onion and garlic for 5–6 minutes, or until softened. Add the wine and puréed tomato and stir through. Simmer for 3–4 minutes, then add any reserved crab liquid. Simmer for another 3–4 minutes. Add the crab meat and season with salt and freshly ground black pepper. Simmer for 5 minutes, or until thick. Discard the garlic.

Preheat the oven to 210°C (415°F/Gas 6–7). Rinse out and dry the crab shells. Spoon the crab mixture into the shells, levelling the surface. Combine the breadcrumbs and parsley and sprinkle over the top. Dot with butter and bake for 6–8 minutes, or until the butter melts and the breadcrumbs brown. Serve hot.

Pick out the cooked crab meat from the legs and body.

Sprinkle the breadcrumbs and parsley over the shells and bake.

plains and mountains

Let's admit it. While Spain's modern cooking, la nueva cocina, is lauded by many as the world's most exciting cuisine today, most of us are more than happy with the simple and satisfying home-style cooking that is found throughout Spain. If you turn your back on the teeming cities and tourist towns along the coast and head for the hills you will discover a surprising truth. No country in Europe has so much wilderness, so many rugged mountain ranges. In Asturias, for example, the Picos de Europa, Europe's largest national park, is a mountain range comprising three towering massifs, divided by gorges only 15 kilometres (9.3 miles) from the coast. Meandering through the Picos are cold clear rivers filled with trout and salmon, when in season, and villages still so remote as to be cut off from car access. So wild is this region that wolves are a continuing problem for livestock farmers.

Half an hour from Madrid begins the Sierra de Guadarrama; behind Gerona lie the mountains of the Cantabrian Range; and south of Granada is the Sierra Nevada, with the highest mountains in Europe, reaching nearly 3500 metres (11,480 feet). Driving along these precipitous mountain roads, you see a sign on many farm gates: coto de caza (hunting reserve). In these private reserves, men hunt partridge, pheasant, woodcock, hare and wild boar. And not just for the sport, but also for the table. The Spanish repertoire is heavy with recipes for game, such as morteruelo (partridge and hare stew) and codornices con aceitunas (quail with olives).

And not just animals are hunted in those mountain passes. The damp forests of Galicia, Navarra and the Basque country are alive with various wild mushrooms in season. You'll find an abundance of morels, chanterelles and ceps, all with local names.

Mountain dishes are different in more ways than just the type of ingredient. Clambering up and down all day creates gargantuan appetites, and dishes to satisfy them. Your first proper fabada asturiana (a stew of the local faba beans, chorizo, morcilla, pig's ear and hocks, eaten in the Picos) will leave you stunned and, well, very full. There is also the lip-smacking, rib-tickling cocido madrileño, not so much a dish as an entire meal, consisting of a soup and meat course, served separately — both with a glass of ink-black tempranillo from the Ribero del Duero. And, if you really love your beef, seek out the restaurants near the bull rings that specialize in cuts of fighting bulls. Once there, you must try the famous stew, rabo de toro. And yes, you can eat the testicles, deep-fried.

gazpacho .... serves 4

THE ANDALUSIANS HAVE DEVISED MANY WAYS TO DEAL WITH THE SEARING HEAT OF THEIR SUMMERS, NOT THE LEAST OF THEM, THE COLD SOUP. GAZPACHO, THE MOST FAMOUS OF THESE WONDERFULLY REFRESHING SOUPS IS SIMPLICITY ITSELF TO MAKE — AND EVEN EASIER TO EAT.

vine-ripened tomatoes	1 kg (2 lb 4 oz)
day-old white crusty bread	2 slices, crusts removed, broken into pieces
red capsicum (pepper)	1, seeded and roughly chopped
garlic	2 cloves, chopped
small green chilli	1, chopped, optional
sugar	1 teaspoon
red wine vinegar	2 tablespoons
extra virgin olive oil	2 tablespoons

garnish

Lebanese (short) cucumber	1/2, seeded and finely diced
red capsicum (pepper)	1/2, seeded and finely diced
green capsicum (pepper)	1/2, seeded and finely diced
red onion	1/2, finely diced
vine-ripened tomato	1/2, diced

Score a cross in the base of each tomato. Put in a bowl of boiling water for 10 seconds, then plunge into cold water and peel away the skin from the cross. Cut the tomatoes in half and scoop out the seeds with a teaspoon. Chop the tomato flesh.

Soak the bread in cold water for 5 minutes, then squeeze out any excess liquid. Put the bread in a food processor with the tomato, capsicum, garlic, chilli, sugar and red wine vinegar and process until combined and smooth.

With the motor running, add the oil to make a smooth, creamy mixture. Season to taste. Refrigerate for at least 2 hours. Add a little extra vinegar, if desired.

To make the garnish, mix together the ingredients. Spoon the chilled gazpacho into soup bowls, top with a little of the garnish and serve the remaining garnish in separate bowls on the side to add as desired.

Soak the bread briefly in water, then squeeze out excess liquid.

Prepare the cucumber for the garnish by seeding it, then dicing.

ajo blanco . . . . serves 4 to 6

YOUR FIRST ENCOUNTER WITH THIS COOL, SILKY-SMOOTH SOUP WITH PALE GREEN GRAPES AND CROUTONS FLOATING ON TOP WILL ASTONISH AND DELIGHT YOU. IT IS ANOTHER SURVIVOR FROM THE MEDIEVAL MOORISH CUISINE OF THE MEDITERRANEAN, WITH ITS CHARACTERISTIC USE OF GROUND ALMONDS TO THICKEN IT.

day-old white crusty bread	200 g (7 oz), crusts removed
whole blanched almonds	150 g (5½ oz/1 cup)
garlic	3–4 cloves, chopped
extra virgin olive oil	125 ml (4 fl oz/½ cup), plus 2 tablespoons, extra
sherry or white wine vinegar	80 ml (2½ fl oz/⅓ cup)
vegetable stock	325–375 ml (11–13 fl oz/ 1¼–1½ cups)
sea salt	to season
day-old white crusty bread	80 g (2¾ oz), extra, crusts removed and cut into 1 cm (½ inch) cubes
seedless green grapes	200 g (7 oz) small

Soak the bread in cold water for 5 minutes, then squeeze out any excess liquid. Put the almonds and garlic in a food processor and process until ground. Add the bread and process until smooth.

With the motor running, add the oil in a steady slow stream until the mixture is the consistency of thick mayonnaise (add a little water if the mixture is too thick). Slowly add the sherry or vinegar and 325 ml (11 fl oz/1¼ cups) of the stock. Blend for 1 minute. Season with sea salt. Refrigerate for at least 2 hours. The soup thickens on refrigeration so you may need to add stock or water to thin it.

When ready to serve, heat the extra oil in a frying pan, add the extra bread cubes and toss over medium heat for 2–3 minutes, or until golden. Drain on paper towels. Serve the soup very cold. Garnish with the grapes and bread cubes.

Although usually called ajo blanco de Malaga, this soup is just as common in the city of Córdoba, once the capital of al-Andalus, and the centre of Moorish culture. There are some pitfalls to avoid when making these cold Andalusian soups. Firstly, never add ice cubes. The extra virgin olive oil and vegetable juices form an emulsion with the cold water, which provides texture, and the melting ice cubes would interfere with that texture, leaving suspicious pools of water on the soup. When making gazpacho, use only ripe, red tomatoes, not tomato paste. And neither gazpacho nor ajo blanco need any spices other than sea salt.

jamón

There is often confusion over what is the difference between jamón and prosciutto. Most importantly, true jamón is made from the flesh of the Iberian pig, the famous pata negra (black foot, so named for its black coat), an animal whose recent revival has ensured the continuity of the magnificent jamónes of Spain.

The Iberian pig's natural habitat is the dehesa, the sparse Mediterranean woodlands populated by oak and holm oak trees. Iberian hams include Denominación de Origen (DO) products from Jabugo, Teruel, Dehesa de Extremadura, Guijuelo, and Huelva.

Serrano is the name given to any ham made not from the flesh of the pata negra, but from white-coated pigs. The best of these hams are serrano consorcio and serrano especial, and those from the town of Trevélez in the Alpujarras.

The second difference between jamón and prosciutto is the curing. Prosciutto is rubbed with salt, while jamón is packed in salt for several months, then hung and air-cured in the dry mountain air for up to three years. A slice of three-year-old Jabugo Gran Reserva with a glass of old amontillado sherry is one of life's great food experiences.

Of course not all pork is turned into ham. Much of it is used in making embutidos — smallgoods of various sorts, cured and fresh. There are countless regional smallgoods of Spain, the best known and best travelled being chorizo, made of chopped or minced (ground) pork and either sweet or hot pimentón (paprika), garlic and black pepper. It is sold dried, for slicing and using as you would salami, or fresh for cooking in various dishes, most commonly with beans.

In Catalonia you will find botifarra blanca, a coarse white pork sausage seasoned with pepper, and botifarra negra, a sausage made of pig's blood, pork fat, some lean meat and mild seasonings. Morcilla, a blood pudding from Asturias, is made using pig's blood mixed with either rice or onion and often fennel, anise and pine nuts. It is an essential ingredient in fabada, the Asturian meat and bean stew.

Everywhere you will find salchicha (fresh pork sausage in links) and salsichón, a hard, cured sausage called longaniza (or fuet if long and thin).

caldo gallego

SIMPLY MEANING GALICIAN BROTH, THIS DISH IS SERVED AND COOKED IN ALL GALICIAN RESTAURANTS, AND IN MOST GALICIAN HOMES DURING WINTER. IT CAN ACCOMMODATE AS MANY DIFFERENT INGREDIENTS AS THERE ARE COOKS MAKING IT. THIS VERSION WOULD BE INSTANTLY RECOGNIZED — AND ENJOYED — IN ITS HOME REGION.

white haricot beans, such as navy beans	250 g (9 oz/1¼ cups)
smoked ham hock	500 g (1 lb 2 oz)
olive oil	2 tablespoons
leek	1, washed and chopped
garlic	1 clove, chopped
pork babyback or American-style ribs	500 g (1 lb 2 oz), separated into 5 cm (2 inch) widths
potatoes	2, peeled and cubed
bay leaf	1
silverbeet (Swiss chard)	1 kg (2 lb 4 oz/1 bunch), washed well and chopped

Rinse the beans, then soak them in cold water for at least 5 hours. Put the ham hock in a large heavy-based saucepan and cover with cold water. Bring to the boil, then reduce the heat and simmer for about 1 hour, or until the meat starts to come away from the bone and is tender. Allow the hock to cool. When cool enough to handle, remove the meat from the bone and cut into 2 cm (³/₄ inch) cubes. Reserve 625 ml (22 fl oz/2½ cups) of the cooking liquid.

Meanwhile, put the beans in a large saucepan and cover with cold water. Bring to the boil, then reduce the heat and simmer for 30 minutes, or until tender. Drain, reserving 250 ml (9 fl oz/1 cup) of the cooking liquid.

Heat the olive oil in a large heavy-based saucepan over medium heat and cook the leek and garlic for about 5 minutes, or until translucent. Add the ham, beans, ribs, potato, bay leaf and reserved cups of cooking liquid (you need to make sure the food is covered with liquid).

Bring to the boil, then reduce the heat, cover and simmer for 45 minutes. Stir in the silverbeet and cook for a further 5 minutes. Season before serving.

Prepare the beans by rinsing, then soaking them in cold water.

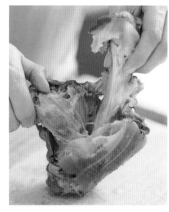

Remove the cooked meat from the bone and cut into cubes.

cocido madrileño . . . . serves 6 to 8

A COCIDO CAN — AND USUALLY DOES — CONTAIN ANY TYPE OF MEAT TO HAND, PLUS CHICKPEAS. THE ONE NECESSARY CONSTANT, ACCORDING TO THE OLD SONG, COCIDITO MADRILEÑO (LITTLE STEW FROM MADRID), IS, '...ALL THE CHARM AND THE SPICE/THAT A WOMAN'S LOVE PUTS RIGHT/INTO THE COCIDITO MADRILEÑO'.

dried chickpeas	225 g (8 oz/1 cup)
chicken	1 kg (2 lb 4 oz), trussed
beef brisket	500 g (1 lb 2 oz), in one piece
smoke-cured bacon	250 g (9 oz) piece
tocino, streaky bacon or speck	125 g (4½ oz)
pig's trotter	1
chorizo	200 g (7 oz)
onion	1, studded with 2 cloves
bay leaf	1
morcilla blood sausage	1, optional
green beans	250 g (9 oz), trimmed and sliced lengthways
green cabbage	250 g (9 oz), cut into sections through the heart
silverbeet (Swiss chard) leaves	300 g (10½ oz), washed well and stalks removed
potatoes	4 small
leeks	2, cut into 10 cm (4 inch) lengths
saffron threads	a pinch
dried rice vermicelli	80 g (2¾ oz)

Soak the chickpeas in cold water overnight. Drain and rinse. Tie loosely in a muslin bag.

Put 3 litres (105 fl oz/12 cups) cold water in a very large deep saucepan. Add the chicken, beef, bacon and tocino and bring to the boil. Add the chickpeas, pig's trotter and chorizo, return to the boil, then add the onion, bay leaf and ½ teaspoon salt. Simmer, partially covered, for 2½ hours (skim the surface if necessary).

After 2 hours, bring a saucepan of water to the boil, add the morcilla, if using, and gently boil for 5 minutes. Drain and set aside. Tie the green beans loosely in a muslin bag. Pour 1 litre (35 fl oz/4 cups) water into the saucepan and bring to the boil. Add the cabbage, silverbeet, potatoes, leek and saffron with 1 teaspoon salt. Return to the boil and simmer for 30 minutes. Add the green beans in the last 10 minutes of cooking.

Strain the stock from both the meat and vegetable pans and combine in a large saucepan. Bring to the boil, adjust the seasoning and stir in the vermicelli. Simmer for 6–7 minutes. Release the chickpeas and pile them in the centre of a large warm platter. Discard the tocino, then slice the meats and sausages. Arrange in groups around the chickpeas at one end of the platter. Release the beans. Arrange the vegetables in groups around the other end. Spoon a little of the simmering broth (minus the vermicelli) over the meat, then pour the rest into a soup tureen, along with the vermicelli. Serve at once. It is traditional to serve both dishes together, although the broth is eaten first.

three ways with pulses

OF ALL THE PULSES USED IN SPANISH COOKING, THE GARBANZO (CHICKPEA) IS THE MOST IMPORTANT. EASILY GROWN ON ARID LAND, IT PROVIDES AFFORDABLE FLAVOUR AND NOURISHMENT, AND IS HIGHLY VERSATILE. ANOTHER IMPORTANT PULSE, ONE DIFFICULT TO FIND OUTSIDE SPAIN, IS THE ASTURIAN FABA, USED IN THE FABADA ASTURIANA. IF YOU CAN'T FIND FABAS, USE ANY WHITE BEAN (IN SPANISH, ALUBIA). LENTEJAS (LENTILS), HERE TEAMED WITH CHORIZO, ARE WIDELY USED RIGHT AROUND THE MEDITERRANEAN.

stewed lentils with chorizo

Rinse 400 g (14 oz) green lentils, then cover with cold water and soak for 2 hours. Heat 1 tablespoon olive oil in a large saucepan over medium heat and add 2 crushed garlic cloves, 1 seeded and diced green capsicum (pepper) and 1 chopped onion. Cook for 5 minutes, or until translucent. Add the drained lentils, 2 teaspoons sweet pimentón (paprika), 1 bay leaf and about 3 tablespoons olive oil. Cover with water, bring to the boil, then reduce the heat and gently simmer for 30 minutes, or until tender. Meanwhile, heat 1 tablespoon olive oil in a frying pan. Add 2 finely sliced bacon rashers, 200 g (7 oz) sliced chorizo and another chopped onion and fry until golden. Add to the lentil mixture with 1 chopped vine-ripened tomato and a large pinch of salt and cook for another 5 minutes. Drizzle a little extra virgin olive oil over the top and serve. Serves 4.

chickpeas and silverbeet

Soak 250 g (9 oz) chickpeas in water overnight. Drain and rinse the chickpeas and put in a large saucepan with 1 diced carrot, 1 flat-leaf (Italian) parsley sprig, 1 bay leaf and 1 chopped onion. Cover with 750 ml (26 fl oz/3 cups) water, bring to the boil and cook for about 20 minutes, or until the chickpeas are almost tender. Add 2 teaspoons salt and 2 tablespoons extra virgin olive oil and cook for 10 minutes. Heat another 2 tablespoons oil in a frying pan and add 1 chopped garlic clove and 1 chopped onion and cook briefly. Add 2 chopped tomatoes and cook for 5 minutes. Stir the tomato mixture and 250 g (9 oz) washed and chopped silverbeet (Swiss chard) into the chickpea mixture (it should be wet enough to be saucy but not too soupy). Cook for 5 minutes, or until the silverbeet is tender. Season well and serve garnished with 2 hard-boiled eggs. Serves 4.

fabada asturiana

Rinse 400 g (14 oz) white haricot beans (such as navy beans) and soak them overnight in cold water. Put 700 g (1 lb 9 oz) smoked ham hock in a large saucepan and cover with water. Bring to the boil, then reduce the heat and simmer for at least 1 hour, or until the meat is tender and starting to come away from the bone. Cool, then remove the meat from the bone and cut into 2 cm (3/4 inch) cubes. Reserve 1 litre (35 fl oz/4 cups) of the cooking liquid. Heat 2 tablespoons olive oil in a large heavy-based saucepan and add 150 g (5 1/2 oz) chopped streaky bacon, 1 chopped brown onion and 2 chopped garlic cloves. Cook for 5 minutes, or until translucent. Add the beans, cubed ham, a pinch of saffron threads, 1 teaspoon sweet pimentón (paprika) and 1 bay leaf and season with salt and freshly ground black pepper. Add the reserved cooking liquid, bring to the boil, then reduce the heat and simmer for at least 1 hour, or until the beans are cooked (they should be soft but not mushy). Add 200 g (7 oz) each of sliced blood sausage (preferably morcilla) and chorizo. Cook for 5 minutes, or until heated through. Season before serving. Serves 4.

gypsy stew..serves 4

THE GYPSIES, OR GITANOS, HAVE BEEN AN IMPORTANT PART OF SPAIN'S CULTURAL LIFE FOR HUNDREDS OF YEARS. THERE ARE VARIOUS DISHES LIKE THIS ONE (USUALLY MEATLESS), ALL CALLED OLLA GITANA. WHY THEY ARE NAMED AFTER THEM IS, LIKE MUCH ABOUT THE GYPSIES, A MYSTERY. NO MATTER, JUST EAT; IT'S DELICIOUS.

white haricot beans, such as navy beans	250 g (9 oz/1¼ cups)
olive oil	80 ml (2½ fl oz/⅓ cup)
garlic	2 cloves, chopped
onions	2, chopped
sweet pimentón (paprika)	1 teaspoon
smoked pimentón (paprika)	1 teaspoon
ground cumin	2 teaspoons
ground cinnamon	¼ teaspoon
cayenne pepper	¼ teaspoon
dried rosemary	1 teaspoon
red capsicum (pepper)	1, seeded and diced
pork tenderloin	750 g (1 lb 10 oz), cut into dice
chopped tomatoes	400 g (14 oz) can
chicken stock	250 ml (9 fl oz/1 cup)
firm potato or orange sweet potato	300 g (10½ oz), peeled and cut into large dice
silverbeet (Swiss chard)	60 g (2¼ oz), washed well and shredded

Cover the beans with cold water and soak for at least 3 hours. Drain well. Preheat the oven to 160°C (315°F/Gas 2–3). Heat 2 tablespoons of the oil in a large saucepan over medium heat, add half the garlic and half the onion and cook for 5 minutes, or until soft. Add the beans and cover with water. Bring to the boil, then reduce the heat and simmer for 45 minutes, or until the beans are soft, but not mushy.

Meanwhile, heat the remaining oil in a large flameproof casserole dish over medium heat. Add the remaining garlic and onion and cook for 5 minutes, or until translucent. Stir through the spices, rosemary, capsicum and diced pork and cook until the pork is pale brown all over. Add the tomato and stock, bring to the boil, then cover and cook in the oven for about 1 hour. Add the beans and sweet potato, top up with 250 ml (9 fl oz/1 cup) water and return to the oven for 30 minutes, or until the sweet potato is tender. Stir in the silverbeet and cook for 5 minutes, or until the silverbeet is wilted. Season to taste before serving.

Beans such as haricot are an important part of the Spanish diet, especially in the north of the country. In particular, the country stews are full of beans, beans whose names change as you cross borders or switch towns. For example, the haba, or the broad (fava) bean, is used throughout Spain, while more or less the same bean, only grown locally, is the Asturian faba. This is the king of beans, the star of the famed fabada Asturiana, and the market for fabas is conducted like a truffle market, with expert buyers and wily sellers eyeing each other off and trying to top one another. When choosing beans for Spanish dishes, choose ones that will stay firm throughout lengthy cooking.

caldereta del condado

THIS LAMB STEW IS FROM THE HUELVA DEHESA, THE SPARSE MEDITERRANEAN WOODLANDS OF THE HUELVA REGION. FOR HUNDREDS OF YEARS THE IBERIAN PIGS AND SHEEP HAVE ROAMED HERE AND THE ORIGINS OF THIS DISH CAN BE TRACED BACK TO THE TRADITIONAL FOOD OF THE SHEPHERDS OF THE REGION.

olive oil	2 tablespoons
onion	1, cut into large dice
carrot	1, cut into large dice
red capsicum (pepper)	1, seeded and cut into large dice
garlic	2 cloves, chopped
lamb leg	1 kg (2 lb 4 oz), boned and cut into 2 cm (³/4 inch) cubes
ham bone or trimmings	1
chopped tomatoes	400 g (14 oz) can
flat-leaf (Italian) parsley	2 tablespoons chopped
mint	2 tablespoons chopped
tomato paste (purée)	2 tablespoons
bay leaves	2
white wine	250 ml (9 fl oz/1 cup)
ground cumin	1 teaspoon
sweet pimentón (paprika)	1 teaspoon
dry breadcrumbs	25 g (1 oz/¹/4 cup)
ground cinnamon	¹/2 teaspoon

Preheat the oven to 180°C (350°F/Gas 4). Heat the olive oil in a large flameproof casserole dish over medium heat and cook the onion, carrot, capsicum and garlic until softened. Add the lamb cubes, ham bone or trimmings, the tomato, parsley, mint, tomato paste, bay leaves, white wine and 185 ml (6 fl oz/³/4 cup) water. Bring to the boil, then cover and bake for 1–1¹/2 hours, or until the lamb is meltingly tender.

Meanwhile, combine the cumin, pimentón, dry breadcrumbs, cinnamon and a pinch of freshly ground black pepper.

Remove the lamb from the casserole dish with a slotted spoon or tongs and set aside. Discard the bay leaves and ham bone. Purée the remaining liquid and vegetables, then stir in the breadcrumb mixture. Cook, stirring, for about 10 minutes, or until the sauce has thickened. Return the lamb to the casserole and gently warm through. Serve with green beans.

When very tender, remove the lamb from the casserole dish.

Add the breadcrumb mixture to the sauce and cook until thick.

cochifrito .... serves 4 to 6

WHAT THE SPANISH PEOPLE EAT TODAY IS VERY MUCH WHAT THEY HAVE EATEN FOR HUNDREDS OF YEARS. A BOWL OF FILLING, TASTY COCHIFRITO, SERVED ON A WINTER'S NIGHT IN FRONT OF A WARM FIRE WITH BREAD AND A GLASS OF LOCALLY-MADE WINE, IS AS APPEALING NOW AS IT EVER WAS.

olive oil	80 ml (2¹/₂ fl oz/¹/₃ cup)
lamb shoulder	1 kg (2 lb 4 oz), diced
onion	1 large, finely chopped
garlic	4 cloves, crushed
sweet pimentón (paprika)	2 teaspoons
lemon juice	80 ml (2¹/₂ fl oz/¹/₃ cup), plus
	1 tablespoon, extra
flat-leaf (Italian) parsley	2 tablespoons

Heat the oil in a large, heavy-based deep frying pan over high heat and cook the lamb in 2 batches for 5 minutes each batch, or until well browned. Remove all the lamb from the pan.

Add the onion to the pan and cook for 4–5 minutes, or until soft and golden. Stir in the garlic and paprika and cook for 1 minute. Return the lamb to the pan with the lemon juice and 1.75 litres (61 fl oz/7 cups) water. Gently simmer over low heat, stirring occasionally, for 2 hours, or until the liquid has almost evaporated and the oil starts to reappear. Stir in the parsley and the extra lemon juice, season with salt and freshly ground black pepper and serve.

Cook the lamb cubes over high heat until brown all over.

Add the pimentón to the onion and garlic and cook until golden.

tripe with chickpeas.. serves 4

LIKE MANY SOUTHERN EUROPEANS, THE SPANISH LOVE THEIR OFFAL, AND FOR THOSE NEW TO THE CUTS, THIS CLASSIC STEW IS A GOOD BEGINNING. THE TRIPE TAKES ON THE STRONG AND HEARTY FLAVOURS OF THE CHORIZO, PIMENTÓN AND GARLIC, THICKENING THE SAUCE AND BINDING THE WHOLE TO THE NUTTY CHICKPEAS.

dried chickpeas	350 g (12 oz)
honeycomb tripe	800 g (1 lb 12 oz), bleached and parboiled
olive oil	170 ml (5½ fl oz/⅔ cup)
onions	2, chopped
garlic	6 cloves, crushed
sweet pimentón (paprika)	2 tablespoons
chorizo	250 g (9 oz), sliced
white wine (Spanish if possible)	300 ml (10½ fl oz)
chopped tomatoes	400 g (14 oz) can
thyme	2 tablespoons chopped
tomato paste (purée)	2 tablespoons
long green chillies	2, chopped
bay leaves	2
cloves	8
nutmeg	a pinch
black peppercorns	20
morcilla blood sausage	200 g (7 oz), sliced
flat-leaf (Italian) parsley	1 large handful, chopped

Soak the chickpeas overnight in cold water. Drain and rinse, then transfer to a saucepan and cover with fresh water. Bring to the boil over high heat and simmer for about 30 minutes, or until tender. Drain and rinse in cold water. Preheat the oven to 160°C (315°F/Gas 2–3).

Soak the tripe for 10 minutes in water, then rinse and drain. Cut into 5 cm (2 inch) squares. Heat the oil in a large flameproof casserole dish over medium heat and cook the onion and garlic for about 5 minutes, or until translucent. Stir in the tripe, pimentón, chorizo and white wine. Bring to the boil and add the chopped tomato, thyme, tomato paste, chilli, bay leaves, cloves, nutmeg, peppercorns and salt to taste. Stir in the blood sausage and cook, covered, in the oven for 1½–2 hours, or until the tripe is tender.

Remove the bay leaves from the casserole, add the chickpeas and cook, covered, for a further 10 minutes. Serve garnished with the chopped parsley.

The taste for offal has been sadly lost by many English-speaking peoples. As this dish shows, however, there is good reason to overcome this prejudice and give the variety meats (as they are more correctly called) a chance. In a Spanish kitchen, everything is used: pig ears and trotters are to be found in a fabada, adding to the richness and thickness of the dish in the same way tripe does; kidneys (riñones) are seared quickly, then put back in a pan and deglazed with fino sherry; and in Majorca, the great speciality is frit, a fry-up of the heart, liver and lungs of the Easter lamb, with onion, chilli and red capsicum (pepper) added. This dish, once tried, will convert even the most timid.

three ways with chicken

THE SPANISH COUNTRY CHICKEN IS DISAPPEARING, BEING REPLACED BY PLUMP BIRDS RAISED IN FACTORY FARMS. ONCE UPON A TIME, YOU COULD BUY CHICKENS WITH SKINS ORANGE FROM PECKING ON THE FALLEN FRUIT FROM THE ORCHARDS THEY GRAZED IN, AND OTHER CHICKENS ENRICHED WITH THE OLIVES FROM THE OLIVE GROVES. THESE THREE RECIPES WOULD BENEFIT FROM BEING MADE WITH FREE-RANGE, IDEALLY ORGANIC, CHICKENS FROM SMALL PRODUCERS.

pollo relleno

Preheat the oven to 200ºC (400ºF/Gas 6). Mix together 100 g (3½ oz) chopped ham or bacon, 100 g (3½ oz) minced (ground) pork, 2 tablespoons chopped flat-leaf (Italian) parsley, 1 crushed garlic clove, a pinch of nutmeg, ½ finely diced onion, 1 teaspoon finely chopped oregano and 2 tablespoons lemon juice. Add 1 beaten egg and mix with your hands until thoroughly combined. Season well. Wash and pat dry a 1.6 kg (3 lb 8 oz) chicken inside and out, then fill the cavity with the stuffing. Tie the legs together and put the chicken in a baking tray, coating it with 2 tablespoons olive oil. Season with salt and freshly ground black pepper and roast for 30 minutes. Reduce the heat to 180ºC (350ºF/Gas 4) and cook for 35–40 minutes, or until the juices run clear when the chicken is pierced between the thigh and body. Allow to rest for 10–15 minutes before carving. Serve a little of the stuffing with each portion of chicken. Serves 4.

chicken cooked with beer

Combine 350 ml (12 fl oz) beer (Spanish or Mexican if possible), 1 tablespoon Dijon mustard, 1 teaspoon sweet pimentón (paprika), 1 diced brown onion, 1 crushed garlic clove and a large pinch of salt. Add 1.2 kg (2 lb 12 oz) chicken pieces, toss until well coated and marinate overnight in the refrigerator. Preheat the oven to 180°C (350°F/Gas 4). Heat 2 tablespoons olive oil in a large flameproof casserole dish over medium heat, add 1 seeded and diced green capsicum (pepper), 1 diced brown onion and 1 crushed garlic clove and cook for 10 minutes, or until softened. Stir in the chicken, marinade and 400 g (14 oz) can chopped tomatoes and season well. Cover and bake for 45–60 minutes, or until the chicken is tender. Serves 4.

chicken with samfaina sauce

Cut 1.5 kg (3 lb 5 oz) chicken into 8 pieces and season with salt and freshly ground black pepper. Heat 60 ml (2 fl oz/¼ cup) olive oil in a large heavy-based saucepan over medium heat, add the chicken in batches and brown well on all sides. Remove the chicken from the pan and reduce the heat to medium–low. Add 2 chopped large brown onions and cook for about 10 minutes, or until translucent. Peel 400 g (14 oz) eggplant (aubergine) and cut into 2 cm (¾ inch) cubes. Cut 350 g (12 oz) zucchini (courgettes) into strips. Cut 2 seeded green or red capsicums (peppers) into 1 cm (½ inch) strips. Add the eggplant, zucchini and capsicums to the pan, along with 3 crushed garlic cloves, and cook for 10 minutes, or until the vegetables are softened. Stir in two 400 g (14 oz) cans chopped tomatoes, 1 bay leaf, 2 tablespoons roughly chopped herbs (such as thyme, oregano and flat-leaf (Italian) parsley) and 125 ml (4 fl oz/½ cup) white wine. Return the chicken pieces to the pan. Bring to the boil, then cover and simmer over low heat for about 45 minutes, or until the chicken is tender and the eggplant is soft. Season well with salt and pepper before serving. Serves 4.

pato con peras .... serves 4

THIS CATALAN FAVOURITE WOULD MOST LIKELY BE MADE USING THE DUCK FARMED IN THE AMPURDAN REGION, THE BARBARY OR MUSCOVY DUCK (READILY AVAILABLE FROM MOST GOOD POULTERERS), WHICH ARE LARGE AND HAVE RICH-TASTING MEAT. FOR BEST RESULTS USE AMONTILLADO SHERRY AND VERY FIRM PEARS.

freshly ground nutmeg	1/4 teaspoon
smoked pimentón (paprika)	1/2 teaspoon
ground cloves	a pinch
duck	2 kg (4 lb 8 oz), jointed into 8 pieces
olive oil	1 tablespoon
bay leaf	1
spring onions (scallions)	8, peeled
baby carrots	8, trimmed
garlic	2 cloves, peeled and sliced
rich sweet sherry	80 ml (2 1/2 fl oz/1/3 cup)
thyme	1 sprig
cinnamon stick	1
chicken stock	1 litre (35 fl oz/4 cups)
firm ripe pears	4, halved and cored
whole almonds	60 g (2 1/4 oz), roasted
dark bittersweet chocolate	25 g (1 oz), grated

Preheat the oven to 180°C (350°F/Gas 4). In a small bowl, mix together the nutmeg, pimentón, cloves and a little salt and freshly ground black pepper. Lightly dust the duck pieces with the spice mixture. Heat the oil in a large flameproof casserole dish and, when hot, brown the duck in batches. Remove from the dish.

Leaving a tablespoon of fat in the casserole, drain off the excess. Add the bay leaf, spring onions and carrots. Cook over medium heat for 3–4 minutes, or until lightly browned. Stir in the garlic and cook for a further 2 minutes. Add the sherry and boil for 1 minute to deglaze the casserole. Stir in the thyme, cinnamon stick and stock and return the duck to the casserole.

Bring to the boil, then transfer the casserole to the oven and bake, covered, for 1 hour 10 minutes, turning the duck pieces halfway through cooking time. Put the pears on top of the duck and bake for 20 minutes more.

Meanwhile, finely grind the almonds in a food processor, then combine with the chocolate.

When the duck is cooked, lift the duck pieces and the pears out of the liquid using a slotted spoon and transfer to a serving dish with the carrots, spring onions and cinnamon stick. Keep warm.

Put the casserole on the stovetop and bring the liquid to the boil. Boil for 7–10 minutes, or until the liquid has reduced by half. Add 60 ml (2 fl oz/1/4 cup) of the hot liquid to the ground almonds and chocolate and stir to combine. Whisk the paste into the rest of the sauce to thicken. Season to taste, pour over the duck and serve immediately.

pollo al chilindrón .... serves 4

THE NORTHEASTERN REGION OF ARAGÓN IS HOME TO THIS RICH AND SATISFYING TRADITIONAL CHICKEN DISH. YOU MAY, IF YOU WISH, ADD A SMALL GLASS OF A RED OR WHITE WINE FROM THE REGION A FEW MINUTES BEFORE SERVING — AND DRINK THE REST WITH IT.

vine-ripened tomatoes	6
chicken	1.5 kg (3 lb 5 oz), cut into 8 portions
olive oil	60 ml (2 fl oz/¼ cup)
red onions	2 large, cut into 5 mm (¼ inch) slices
garlic	2 cloves, crushed
red capsicums (peppers)	3, seeded and cut into 1 cm (½ inch) strips
jamón or prosciutto	60 g (2¼ oz), finely chopped
thyme	1 tablespoon chopped
sweet pimentón (paprika)	2 teaspoons
pitted black olives	8
pitted green olives	8

Score a cross in the base of each tomato. Put in a bowl of boiling water for 10 seconds, then plunge into cold water and peel away the skin from the cross. Cut each tomato in half and scoop out the seeds with a teaspoon. Finely chop the flesh.

Pat dry the chicken with paper towels and season well with salt and freshly ground black pepper. Heat the oil in a heavy-based frying pan over medium heat and cook the chicken a few pieces at a time, skin side down, for 4–5 minutes, or until golden. Turn the chicken over and cook for another 2–3 minutes. Transfer to a plate and keep warm.

Add the onion, garlic, capsicum, jamón and thyme to the frying pan. Cook, stirring frequently, for about 10 minutes, or until the vegetables have softened but not browned.

Add the tomato and pimentón, increase the heat and cook for 10–12 minutes, or until the sauce has thickened and reduced. Return the chicken to the pan and coat well with the sauce. Cover the pan and reduce the heat to low. Simmer the chicken for 25–30 minutes, or until tender. Add the olives and adjust the seasoning, if necessary, before serving.

quails in vine leaves .... serves 4

A WIDE VARIETY OF BIRDS ARE USED IN SPANISH COOKING, FROM WELL-FED FARM CHICKENS TO WILD-CAUGHT
PHEASANTS AND EVEN PARTRIDGES, WHICH ARE OFTEN SERVED WITH A RICH CHOCOLATE SAUCE. QUAILS, WITH
THEIR DELICATE-TASTING FLESH, ARE TREATED MORE SIMPLY, HERE PREPARED WITH JAMÓN AND SHERRY.

quails	8
lemons	2
jamón or prosciutto	8 slices
vine leaves	16, in brine, rinsed in cold water
olive oil	1 tablespoon
veal or chicken stock	60 ml (2 fl oz/¼ cup)
sweet sherry	100 ml (3½ fl oz)
butter	50 g (1¾ oz) cold, diced
watercress	250 g (9 oz/½ bunch)

Preheat the oven to 200°C (400°F/Gas 6). Wash the quails and pat dry with paper towels. Cut the lemons into quarters and put a quarter inside each quail cavity. Season and wrap each quail with a slice of jamón. Put a quail on top of 2 overlapping vine leaves, fold the leaves around the bird and secure with kitchen twine. Repeat with the remaining quails and leaves.

Put the wrapped quails on an oven tray, drizzle with the oil and bake for 30 minutes. Remove from the oven and pierce a quail between the thigh and body through to the bone and check that the juices run out clear. If they are pink, return to the oven and cook for another 5 minutes. Transfer the quails to a separate plate to rest for 10 minutes, removing the twine and vine leaves.

Pour the remaining pan juices into a small saucepan with the stock and sherry. Bring to the boil and gradually whisk in the butter, whisking for 3 minutes, or until the sauce is slightly glazy. Serve the quail on a bed of watercress, drizzled with the sauce.

Put a lemon wedge in the cavity, then wrap the quail with jamón.

Use two vine leaves to wrap each quail, overlapping to cover.

Secure the quail and its wrapping with kitchen twine.

three ways with wine

SPANISH WINE IS FINALLY REVEALING ITSELF TO THE REST OF THE WORLD. THE BLEND OF TECHNOLOGY AND TRADITION, AS WELL AS THE WIDE VARIETY OF SOILS, SITES AND MICROCLIMATES, PRODUCES WINES OF EXCEPTIONAL QUALITY. WINES RANGE FROM THE TIMELESS SHERRIES AND THOSE MADE USING INDIGENOUS SPANISH GRAPE VARIETIES (SUCH AS TEMPRANILLO AND ALBARIÑO) TO POWERFUL MODERN WINES MADE USING FRENCH GRAPES LIKE CHARDONNAY. THE RESULT: AN EMBARRASSMENT OF CHOICES FOR THE SPANISH COOK.

roast leg of lamb

Preheat the oven to 200°C (400°F/Gas 6). Rinse 1.5 kg (3 lb 5 oz) leg of lamb and pat dry with paper towels. Put the lamb in a roasting tin and drizzle 2 tablespoons olive oil and 250 ml (9 fl oz/1 cup) white wine (ideally Spanish) over the top. Mix together 150 g (5½ oz/ 1 bunch) chopped flat-leaf (Italian) parsley, 2 teaspoons finely chopped rosemary, 2 teaspoons finely chopped thyme and 8 crushed garlic cloves. Sprinkle over the lamb, pressing down firmly. Put the lamb in the oven and cook for 20 minutes, basting with the tin juices. Reduce the temperature to 180°C (350°F/Gas 4) and cook for 1 hour. Remove from the oven and rest for at least 10 minutes before serving. The lamb will be medium–rare to medium. If you prefer your lamb rare, allow 20–25 minutes cooking time per 500 g (1 lb 2 oz), and for well done 30–35 minutes per 500 g (1 lb 2 oz). Serves 4.

oxtail stew

Preheat the oven to 150°C (300°F/Gas 2). Cut 2 kg (4 lb 8 oz) oxtails into 2 cm (¾ inch) thick pieces. Coat the oxtails with seasoned flour. Heat 2 tablespoons olive oil in a large heavy-based flameproof casserole dish over medium heat, add the oxtails in batches and brown all over. Remove to a plate. Heat another 2 tablespoons olive oil in the casserole over medium heat, add 2 chopped brown onions, 1 diced leek, 2 diced carrots, 1 chopped celery stalk and 2 crushed garlic cloves and cook for about 5 minutes, or until the vegetables are softened. Stir in 400 g (14 oz) can crushed tomatoes, 375 ml (13 fl oz/1½ cups) white wine, 375 ml (13 fl oz/1½ cups) beef stock, 1 teaspoon sweet pimentón (paprika), 1 bay leaf and 2 tablespoons chopped thyme and bring to the boil. Add the oxtails, making sure they are covered with liquid (add extra water if necessary), then cover and bake for 4–5 hours, depending on the size of the oxtails. The meat should easily fall away from the bone when ready. Serve garnished with 2 tablespoons chopped flat-leaf (Italian) parsley. Serves 4–6.

rabbit in red wine

Joint 2 x 1 kg (2 lb 4 oz) rabbits and cut each rabbit into 8 pieces. Season the meat. Heat 60 ml (2 fl oz/¼ cup) olive oil in a heavy flameproof casserole dish over medium heat. Add the rabbit in batches and cook for about 4 minutes per batch, or until golden brown. Remove and set aside. Heat another 30 ml (1 fl oz) oil in the casserole and cook 1 chopped large brown onion for 5 minutes, or until translucent. Add 6 peeled and chopped Roma (plum) tomatoes and simmer gently for 10 minutes. Stir in 1 teaspoon sweet pimentón (paprika), 6 crushed garlic cloves, 3 slices jamón or prosciutto, cut into strips, 100 g (3½ oz) chopped chorizo, 3 seeded and diced red capsicums (peppers), 2 tablespoons chopped thyme, 250 ml (9 fl oz/1 cup) red wine (preferably Spanish), the rabbit pieces and 2 tablespoons roughly chopped flat-leaf (Italian) parsley. Check the seasoning. Bring to the boil, then reduce the heat and simmer for 35 minutes, or until the rabbit is tender. Remove the rabbit pieces and simmer the sauce for 20–30 minutes, or until reduced and glazy. Return the rabbit to the casserole and gently heat through. Season to taste, garnish with a little parsley and serve. Serves 4.

chicken in saffron stew

THIS IS A MODERN DISH, USING ONE OF SPAIN'S NATIVE INGREDIENTS, AZAFRAN (SAFFRON), AND UTILIZING A CLASSIC CATALAN THICKENING AND FLAVOURING TECHNIQUE, THE PICADA. IN THIS RECIPE THE PICADA COMBINES PINE NUTS, CINNAMON, SAFFRON, GARLIC AND PARSLEY.

olive oil	60 ml (2 fl oz/¼ cup)
pine nuts	40 g (1½ oz/¼ cup)
bread	1 thick slice, crusts removed and cut into pieces
ground cinnamon	½ teaspoon
saffron threads	a pinch
garlic	2 cloves
flat-leaf (Italian) parsley	2 tablespoons chopped
chicken	1.5 kg (3 lb 5 oz), cut into 8 pieces and seasoned with salt
brown onions	2, finely chopped
white wine	125 ml (4 fl oz/½ cup)
chicken stock	375 ml (13 fl oz/1½ cups)
bay leaf	1
thyme	2 sprigs
lemon juice	2 tablespoons
egg yolks	2

Heat 1 tablespoon of the oil in a large heavy-based flameproof casserole dish over medium–high heat. Add the pine nuts and bread and lightly fry for about 3 minutes, or until golden. Remove and drain on paper towels. When cooled slightly, put in a mortar or food processor, add the cinnamon, saffron, garlic and half the parsley and pound or process to a coarse, crumbly consistency.

Heat the remainder of the oil in the casserole over medium heat and brown the chicken pieces for about 5 minutes. Remove to a plate. Add the onion to the casserole and cook for 5 minutes, or until translucent.

Return the chicken pieces to the casserole with the wine, stock, bay leaf and thyme and simmer, covered, over medium heat for 1 hour, or until the chicken is tender. Remove the chicken and cover to keep warm. Add the pine nut paste to the casserole and cook for 1 minute. Remove from the heat and whisk in the lemon juice, egg yolks and remaining parsley. Return the casserole to the stovetop and stir over very low heat until just thickened slightly (do not allow it to boil or the sauce will split). Season to taste, return the chicken to the casserole and gently warm through before serving.

Make the picada by pounding the nuts, bread and spices together.

Add the lemon juice, egg and parsley, whisking to incorporate.

chicken with raisins and pine nuts

SOME INGREDIENTS TURN UP IN SPANISH FOOD, TIME AND TIME AGAIN, ALL OVER THE COUNTRY. PINE NUTS AND RAISINS ARE TWO SUCH INGREDIENTS, ALWAYS TOGETHER, LIKE CHORIZO AND GARBANZOS (CHICKPEAS), AND ALWAYS GOOD. IN THIS SIMPLE DISH THEY ADD RICHNESS AND SWEETNESS TO THE CHICKEN.

chicken	1.25 kg (2 lb 12 oz)
lemon	1/2, cut into 2 wedges
bay leaves	2
olive oil	60 ml (2 fl oz/1/4 cup)
onion	1, thinly sliced
garlic	3 cloves, crushed
chopped tomatoes	400 g (14 oz) can
white wine	170 ml (51/2 fl oz/2/3 cup)
sun-dried tomato purée or tomato paste (purée)	2 tablespoons
red or green capsicum (pepper)	1, seeded and cut into thin strips
pitted black olives	40 g (11/2 oz/1/3 cup)
raisins	3 tablespoons
pine nuts	2 tablespoons, roasted

Preheat the oven to 200°C (400°F/Gas 6). Wash and pat dry the chicken, then season with plenty of salt and freshly ground black pepper. Put the lemon wedges and bay leaves inside the cavity, drizzle with 2 tablespoons of the oil and roast in the oven for 1 hour. Pierce the chicken between the thigh and body through to the bone and check that the juices run out clear; if they are pink, cook for another 15 minutes.

Meanwhile, heat the remaining oil in a large frying pan over medium heat and cook the onion and garlic for 5 minutes, or until translucent. Add the tomato and cook for 2 minutes. Stir in the wine, tomato purée, capsicum, olives and raisins and simmer for 6–8 minutes, or until the mixture reaches a sauce consistency. Cut the chicken into 8 portions, tipping the juice from the chicken cavity into the sauce. Spoon the sauce over the chicken pieces and garnish with the pine nuts.

Season the chicken, then fill the cavity with lemon wedges.

Cook the chicken until golden and the juices run out clear.

While the chicken cooks, prepare the tomato sauce.

three ways with vegetables

VEGETABLES ARE TREATED WITH RESPECT IN SPAIN. THE COUNTRYSIDE IS RICH WITH WELL-TENDED MARKET GARDENS, AND IN THE VILLAGES, YOU CAN READ THE SEASONS FROM THE PRODUCE ON DISPLAY: IF THERE ARE CAPSICUMS (PEPPERS), IT MUST BE SUMMER; IF ARTICHOKES AND CAULIFLOWER ABOUND, WINTER HAS ARRIVED. ALL THREE DISHES BELOW CAN BE EATEN AS INTRODUCTIONS TO A MAIN MEAL, OR AS A MEAL IN THEMSELVES. ESCALIVADA, CATALAN CHARGRILLED VEGETABLES, CAN BE FOUND IN RESTAURANTS RIGHT ACROSS SPAIN.

judias verdes en salsa de tomate

Cook 300 g (10½ oz) trimmed green beans in boiling water for 3–5 minutes, or until tender. Drain and set aside. Heat 1 tablespoon olive oil in a frying pan, add 1 finely chopped onion and cook over medium heat for 5 minutes, or until soft. Add 2 finely chopped garlic cloves and cook for 1 minute. Add 1 tablespoon sweet pimentón (paprika), ¼ teaspoon chilli flakes and 1 crushed bay leaf, cook for 1 minute, then stir in 400 g (14 oz) can good-quality crushed tomatoes. Simmer over medium heat for about 15 minutes, or until reduced and pulpy. Add the reserved beans and 2 tablespoons chopped flat-leaf (Italian) parsley and cook for 1 minute, or until warmed through. Season to taste. Serve warm or at room temperature. Serves 4.

escalivada

Without slicing through the base, cut 1 red onion from top to bottom into 6 sections, leaving it attached at the base. Put on a barbecue or on a chargrill pan, with 6 small eggplants (aubergines), about 16 cm (6½ inches) long, 4 red capsicums (peppers) and 4 orange capsicums. Cook over medium heat for 10 minutes, turning occasionally, until the eggplant and capsicum skins are blackened and blistered. Put the capsicums in a plastic bag for 10 minutes to cool. Set aside the onion and eggplant. Dry-fry 1 tablespoon baby capers with a pinch of salt until crisp. Cut the onion into its 6 sections and discard the charred outer skins. Peel the skins off the eggplants and remove the stalks. Cut from top to bottom into slices. Peel the capsicums and remove the seeds. Cut into wide slices. Arrange all the vegetables on a large serving platter. Drizzle over 80 ml (2½ fl oz/⅓ cup) good-quality olive oil and season to taste with salt and freshly ground black pepper. Scatter 1 tablespoon chopped flat-leaf (Italian) parsley, 2 chopped garlic cloves and the capers over the top. Serve cold as a salad or warm as an accompaniment to barbecued meats. Serves 4.

silverbeet with raisins and pine nuts

Trim the stalks from 500 g (1 lb 2 oz) silverbeet (Swiss chard) or English spinach, then wash the leaves and shred them. Put 2 tablespoons pine nuts in a frying pan and stir over medium heat for 3 minutes, or until lightly browned. Remove from the pan and reserve. Heat 1 tablespoon olive oil in the pan, add 1 halved and sliced small red onion and cook over low heat, stirring occasionally, for 10 minutes, or until translucent. Increase the heat to medium, add 1 thinly sliced garlic clove and cook for 1 minute. Add the silverbeet, 2 tablespoons raisins and a pinch of ground cinnamon. Cover and cook for 2 minutes, or until the silverbeet wilts. Stir in the reserved pine nuts, season to taste and serve. Serves 6.

catalan-style cannelloni .... serves 6

CANALONS, AS THEY ARE KNOWN IN CATALONIA, ARE JUST ONE OF THE MANY TYPES OF PASTA USED IN THE AREA. THIS DISH IS TYPICAL OF BARCELONA, AND IS AN ADAPTATION OF THE ORIGINAL BROUGHT BY ITALIAN MIGRANTS WHO CAME TO THE CITY IN THE NINETEENTH CENTURY.

olive oil	2 tablespoons
minced (ground) beef or veal	125 g (4 1/2 oz)
minced (ground) pork	125 g (4 1/2 oz)
chicken livers	200 g (7 oz), chopped
brown onion	1, diced
leek	1, halved lengthways and chopped
dry sherry	2 1/2 tablespoons
thyme	1 tablespoon chopped
crushed tomatoes	400 g (14 oz) can
flat-leaf (Italian) parsley	4 tablespoons chopped
butter	70 g (2 1/2 oz)
plain (all-purpose) flour	60 g (2 1/4 oz/1/2 cup)
milk	1 litre (35 fl oz/4 cups)
nutmeg	a pinch
dried cannelloni tubes	250 g (9 oz) packet
tomato paste (purée) or passata	100 ml (3 1/2 fl oz)
manchego or Parmesan cheese	100 g (3 1/2 oz/1 cup) grated

Preheat the oven to 180°C (350°F/Gas 4). Heat the olive oil in a large heavy-based frying pan over medium heat. Cook the beef, pork, chicken livers, onion and leek for 10 minutes, or until the meat is well browned, breaking up any lumps with the back of a wooden spoon. Add the sherry, thyme, tomato and half the parsley and cook for 3 minutes, or until most of the liquid has evaporated. Season and leave to cool.

Melt the butter in a large saucepan over medium heat. Add the flour and cook, stirring with a wooden spoon, for 1–2 minutes, or until pale yellow. Remove from the heat and add the milk gradually, stirring constantly until blended. Return to the heat and slowly bring the mixture to the boil, whisking for 15 minutes, or until thickened. Season with nutmeg, salt and freshly ground black pepper.

Fill the cannelloni with the meat mixture using a wide-tip piping bag or a spoon. Put the filled cannelloni side by side in a buttered ovenproof dish. Pour the white sauce over the top and dot with the puréed tomato. Top with the grated cheese and bake for 40–45 minutes. Garnish with the remaining chopped parsley.

Use a wooden spoon to break up any lumps in the meat mixture.

Allow the mixture to cool, then use to fill the cannelloni tubes.

fideus a la catalana .... serves 4 to 6

THERE ARE NUMEROUS RECIPES FOR THIS SHORT AND THIN NOODLE, A CURIOSITY OF CATALAN CUISINE. UNLIKE MOST ITALIAN PASTAS, FIDEUS IS VERY SHORT — HALF THE LENGTH OF YOUR LITTLE FINGER — AND THIN, MORE NOODLE THAN SPAGHETTI. BELOW IS A CLASSIC COMBINATION OF FIDEUS WITH PORK.

olive oil	80 ml (2½ fl oz/⅓ cup)
pork spare ribs	250 g (9 oz), cut into 1 cm (½ inch) thick slices
brown onion	1, chopped
tomato paste (purée) or passata	125 ml (4 fl oz/½ cup)
sweet pimentón (paprika)	1 teaspoon
fresh spicy pork sausages	100 g (3½ oz), thickly sliced
chorizo	100 g (3½ oz), cut into pieces
beef or chicken stock	1.5 litres (52 fl oz/6 cups)
fideus or spaghettini	500 g (1 lb 2 oz)
bread	1 slice
nuts, such as hazelnuts, pine nuts or almonds	50 g (1¾ oz/⅓ cup)
garlic	2 cloves, crushed
flat-leaf (Italian) parsley	2 tablespoons chopped
ground cinnamon	¼ teaspoon
saffron threads	¼ teaspoon

Heat the oil in a large heavy-based saucepan over medium–high heat and cook the ribs in batches until golden. Add the onion and cook for 5 minutes, or until softened. Stir in the tomato paste and pimentón and cook for a few minutes more.

Add the spicy sausages, chorizo and the stock (reserving 2 tablespoons) and bring to the boil. Reduce to a simmer and add the fideus or spaghettini (if using spaghettini, break the pasta into 2.5 cm (1 inch) pieces before using). Cook, covered, for 15 minutes, or until the pasta is al dente.

Meanwhile, toast the bread and remove the crusts. In a mortar or food processor, pound or process the nuts with the garlic, parsley, cinnamon and bread to make a paste. Stir in the saffron. If the mixture is too dry, add 1–2 tablespoons of the reserved stock. Stir the cooked pasta into the casserole and simmer for 5 minutes, or until the casserole has thickened slightly. Season well before serving.

According to food scholar Charles Perry, it was not the Italians or even the Romans who bought fideus to Catalonia, but the Moors, who took the idea from the Greeks. Fideus, the original Moorish word, means abundant or overflowing. There is a related Italian pasta, fedelini, which is somewhat like an angel hair pasta. The first mention of fideus was in 1429, almost two hundred years before the appearance of fedelini in Italian recipes. Unlike Italian pasta, fideus is often cooked dry with other ingredients (as opposed to being boiled in water first). If you cannot find fideus, spaghettini is a good substitute.

sofregit

Sofregit is a flavour base used in countless Catalan recipes. Though simple, it requires care and time to perfect. Of course, it is related to the Italian soffritto and the Spanish sofrito, but as the Catalans tend to fuss a little more with all their food, so it is with sofregit.

The onions are the most important ingredient. Mild, sweet onions are best, large red ones are fine. And, although the word sofregit means lightly fried, that is in reference to the level of the flame, not the length of cooking time: the onions should be gently stewed, in an abundance of olive oil, for as long as you have patience. They should be deep brown and caramelized, but definitely not burnt. When finished, pour off the excess oil and reserve for other uses. It goes without saying that you should use the reddest, ripest tomatoes you can find (failing that, and in winter, good-quality canned tomatoes can be used).

Cover the bottom of a large frying pan or flameproof casserole dish with 125–150 ml (4–5 fl oz) extra virgin olive oil. Heat over medium heat for several minutes, then add 3 roughly chopped onions. Stir the onion into the oil, reduce the heat to very low (even using a simmer pad if you have one) and continue cooking until the onion has reached the desired dark caramelized state. Add a little water if it threatens to burn. Tip out and reserve the excess oil once the onion is done.

Peel, seed and chop 6 vine-ripened tomatoes — or use 2 x 400 g (14 oz) can tomatoes — and add to the frying pan or casserole. Continue cooking until the liquid has evaporated and the tomato has begun to dissolve into the onion. At this point, if necessary for a specific recipe, add herbs. If you need garlic, add after the onion has finished cooking. Sofregit can be stored, under a thin layer of oil, in a screw top or sealed container, for up to three weeks in the refrigerator.

tumbet .... serves 6 to 8

THE CLASSIC VEGETABLE DISH OF MAJORCA, TUMBET IS EATEN AS A MEAL IN ITS OWN RIGHT, EITHER HOT OR COLD, OR AS AN ACCOMPANIMENT TO BAKED LAMPUGA (IN ENGLISH, MAHI MAHI OR DOLPHIN FISH) DURING ITS SHORT MEDITERRANEAN AUTUMN SEASON.

olive oil	250 ml (9 fl oz/1 cup)
waxy potatoes, such as desiree, kipfler or Pontiac	500 g (1 lb 2 oz), cut into 5 mm (1/4 inch) rounds
eggplants (aubergines)	500 g (1 lb 2 oz), cut into 5 mm (1/4 inch) rounds
green capsicums (peppers)	500 g (1 lb 2 oz), seeded and cut into 3 cm (1 1/4 inch) pieces
flat-leaf (Italian) parsley	1 large handful, roughly chopped

tomato sauce

vine-ripened tomatoes	1 kg (2 lb 4 oz)
olive oil	2 tablespoons
garlic	3 cloves, crushed
red onion	1, finely chopped
thyme	2 teaspoons chopped

To make the tomato sauce, score a cross in the base of each tomato and put in a bowl of boiling water for 10 seconds. Plunge into cold water and peel the skin away from the cross. Cut each tomato in half and scoop out the seeds with a teaspoon. Finely chop the tomato flesh.

Heat the oil in a heavy-based frying pan and cook the garlic and onion over low heat for 5–6 minutes, or until softened. Increase the heat to medium, add the tomato and thyme and cook for 20 minutes, or until thickened. Season to taste. Preheat the oven to 180°C (350°F/Gas 4).

While the sauce is cooking, heat the oil in a heavy-based frying pan over low heat and cook the potato in batches until tender but not brown. Remove with a slotted spoon or tongs and transfer to a casserole dish measuring about 27 x 21 x 5 cm (10 3/4 x 8 1/4 x 2 inches). Season lightly.

Increase the heat to high and cook the eggplant for 3 minutes each side, or until golden, adding a little more oil if necessary. Drain the slices on paper towels, then arrange on top of the potatoes. Season lightly.

Cook the capsicum in the same pan until tender but not browned, adding a little more olive oil if needed. Remove with a slotted spoon, drain on paper towels and arrange on the eggplant. Season lightly with salt and freshly ground black pepper. Pour the sauce over the top and bake for about 20 minutes. Sprinkle with the parsley and serve warm as an accompaniment to fish or meat, or serve at room temperature with allioli (page 48).

Cook the eggplant slices over high heat until golden.

Drain the cooked capsicum strips, then layer them over the eggplant.

huevos a la flamenca . . . . serves 4

THIS DISH IS ORIGINALLY FROM ANDALUSIA, BUT IS NOW FOUND RIGHT AROUND THE SPANISH PENINSULA. IT IS FULL OF THE COLOUR, GUTSY FLAVOURS AND EXUBERANCE OF THE GYPSIES WHO INVENTED FLAMENCO. SERVE IT WITH A BIG RED FROM ALICANTE.

vine-ripened tomatoes	500 g (1 lb 2 oz)
olive oil	60 ml (2 fl oz/¼ cup)
potatoes	400 g (14 oz), cut into 2 cm (¾ inch) cubes
red capsicum (pepper)	1, seeded and cut into strips
onion	1, chopped
jamón or prosciutto	100 g (3½ oz), thickly sliced
thin green asparagus	150 g (5½ oz), trimmed
fresh or frozen peas	100 g (3½ oz)
baby green beans	100 g (3½ oz), sliced
tomato paste (purée)	2 tablespoons
eggs	4
chorizo	100 g (3½ oz), thinly sliced
flat-leaf (Italian) parsley	2 tablespoons chopped

Score a cross in the base of each tomato. Put in a bowl of boiling water for 10 seconds, then plunge into cold water and peel away the skin from the cross. Roughly chop the tomatoes.

Heat the oil in a large frying pan or saucepan and cook the potato over medium heat for 8 minutes, or until golden. Remove with a slotted spoon. Reduce the heat and add the capsicum and onion to the pan. Cut 2 jamón slices into pieces similar in size to the capsicum and add to the pan. Cook for 6 minutes, or until the onion is soft.

Preheat the oven to 180°C (350°F/Gas 4). Reserve 4 asparagus spears. Add the rest to the pan with the peas, beans, tomato and tomato paste. Add 125 ml (4 fl oz/½ cup) water and season with salt and freshly ground black pepper. Return the potato cubes to the pan. Cover and cook over low heat for about 10 minutes, stirring occasionally.

Grease a large oval ovenproof dish. Transfer the vegetables to the dish, discarding any excess liquid. Using the back of a spoon, make 4 deep, evenly spaced indentations and break an egg into each. Top with the reserved asparagus and the chorizo. Cut the remaining jamón into large pieces and distribute over the top. Sprinkle with the parsley. Bake for about 20 minutes, or until the egg whites are just set. Serve warm.

Return the potato to the pan and cook until the vegetables are soft.

Add the eggs to the dish, nestling them among the vegetables.

queso

The world is discovering Spanish food. And discovering not just the great chefs and dishes, but also the great food products. Even five years ago, many would have been hard-pressed to name more than one Spanish cheese: manchego.

The truth is, Spain produces — officially — one hundred different types of cheese, twelve of which are covered by a Denominación de Origen label. This official number is just the beginning, however. The market at Cangas de Onis in Asturias, for example, could well have thirty different cheeses for sale.

Most of these cheeses are made by hand, by cheesemakers who run their own herds of milking animals. Even a famous cheese like Cabrales, from the Picos de Europa mountains in Asturias, is made by makers in much the same way as it probably was in the time of Pelayo (the legendary eighth century Visigoth and first King of Asturias), with milk from their own herds — often a mixture of cow, goat and sheep. It is matured in mountain caves, where the creamy paste acquires its pungent flavour from wild yeasts.

In Extremadura, in Spain's southwest, you will find the cheese that three Michelin star chef Juan Mari Arzak considers the best in Spain: Torta de la Serena. Made from raw merino milk, it is a ripe, luscious, oozing, sticky, custard-textured centre held (only just) in place by a crusty rind. Scoop it out with a spoon.

One of the finest goat's milk cheeses is the queso de Murcia al vino, from the province of Murcia on the east coast. During ripening, the rind is washed twice weekly with local wines, either Tecla or Jumilla, turning the rind red and giving the cheese a lovely floral bouquet and a rich winey flavour.

And of course there is always manchego (pictured, right), the best known of Spain's cheeses, made only from sheep's milk in the provinces of Toledo, Cuenca, Albacete and Ciudad. The best is nutty and sweet with great palate length. From its provincial homes, manchego travels around Spain, and the world. Afuega'l Pitu del Aramo, on the other hand, rarely leaves Temia in Asturias. The name of this tart, dense cow's milk cheese means, in the Asturian dialect, 'choke the chicken of Aramo', indicating the method for testing the curd. In ancient times a small amount of the curd was given to an unfortunate chicken who choked if it was ready. This is possibly the most ancient cheese produced in Spain but, thankfully, the testing methods have changed somewhat.

andrajos

THE NAME OF THIS ANDALUSIAN DISH MEANS TATTERS AND RAGS, AND PROBABLY REFERS TO THE WAY IN WHICH THE ORIGINAL RECIPES INCLUDED FLOUR AND WATER FOR MAKING LITTLE SQUARE DUMPLINGS (THE RAGS AND TATTERS). THE SAME EFFECT IS CREATED HERE WITH LASAGNE SHEETS. MEAT WAS ALSO OFTEN INCLUDED.

bacalao (salt cod)	500 g (1 lb 2 oz)
olive oil	2 tablespoons
onion	1, chopped
garlic	2 cloves, finely chopped
crushed tomatoes	400 g (14 oz) can
sweet pimentón (paprika)	1/2 teaspoon
smoked pimentón (paprika)	1/2 teaspoon
saffron threads	a pinch
black peppercorns	10
cumin seeds	1 teaspoon
chicken stock	500 ml (17 fl oz/2 cups)
dried lasagne sheets	100 g (3 1/2 oz), cut in half to form squares approximately 9 x 9 cm (3 1/2 x 3 1/2 inches)
flat-leaf (Italian) parsley	2 tablespoons chopped
lemon juice	1 tablespoon

Soak the bacalao in plenty of cold water for about 20 hours, changing the water four or five times to remove excess salt. Drain, then put the bacalao in a large saucepan and cover with cold water. Bring to the boil, then reduce the heat and simmer for 30–45 minutes, or until the fish is soft and able to be removed from the bone. Drain, allow to cool, then shred the bacalao.

Heat the oil in a large, heavy-based flameproof casserole dish over medium heat. Cook the onion and garlic for 5 minutes, or until translucent. Add the crushed tomato and cook for 2 minutes. Stir in the sweet and smoked pimentón and the shredded fish.

In a mortar or food processor, pound or grind the saffron, peppercorns and cumin seeds to a powder. Add to the casserole with the chicken stock and simmer for 15 minutes, or until reduced to a sauce consistency. Meanwhile, cook the lasagne sheets in boiling water until al dente. Stir the lasagne sheets into the casserole and season to taste. Garnish with the parsley, drizzle the lemon juice over the top and serve.

So much Spanish food is red with spicy, sweet and smoky pimentón, known in English by its Hungarian name, paprika. The best pimentón comes from La Vera in Extremadura in western Spain, where it is made using traditional methods: when completely ripe, red capsicums (peppers) are dried, smoked and turned daily for between ten to fifteen days over slow-burning holm oak fires. This results in the characteristically intense smoky aroma and flavour of La Vera pimentón. After smoking, the capsicums are stone ground a total of seven times, which creates a silky texture. This slow and laborious stone grinding also protects the pimentón from its major enemy — bitterness.

pimientos rellenos .... serves 4

MANY VEGETABLE DISHES THOUGHT OF BY NON-SPANIARDS AS 'SIDES' WILL TURN UP IN SPANISH HOMES AS DISHES IN THEIR OWN RIGHT. THIS IS ESPECIALLY TRUE OF THE VEGETABLES OF NAVARRA, IN THE COUNTRY'S NORTH, WHICH ARE FAMED ACROSS SPAIN. FROM LA RIOJA IN THAT PROVINCE, COMES THIS SIMPLE FAVOURITE.

red capsicums (peppers)	4
olive oil	60 ml (2 fl oz/¼ cup)
onion	1, chopped
garlic	2 cloves, chopped
minced (ground) pork or beef	400 g (14 oz)
white wine	125 ml (4 fl oz/½ cup)
chopped tomatoes	400 g (14 oz) can, drained well
long-grain rice	100 g (3½ oz), cooked
egg	1, lightly beaten
flat-leaf (Italian) parsley	2 tablespoons finely chopped

Cut the tops off the capsicums and reserve them to use as lids. Using a small, sharp knife, carefully cut the internal membrane and seeds away from the capsicum and discard. Preheat the oven to 180°C (350°F/Gas 4).

Heat 2 tablespoons of the olive oil in a frying pan over medium–high heat and cook the onion and garlic for 5 minutes, or until lightly golden. Add the pork or beef and brown well. Stir in the wine, then reduce the heat to low and simmer for 10 minutes, or until the wine has been absorbed.

Add the tomato and simmer for a further 10 minutes, then add the rice. Remove from the heat and stir in the beaten egg and parsley. Season well.

Stuff the capsicums with the meat mixture, put the lids on top and stand upright in an ovenproof dish. Drizzle with the remaining olive oil and bake for 45–50 minutes, or until the stuffing is cooked through and the capsicums are tender. Remove from the oven and leave, covered, for about 5 minutes before serving.

Cut the tops off the capsicums and reserve.

Remove the membrane and seeds without cutting the flesh.

Fill the capsicums with the mixture, then replace the tops.

pastries and sweets

Behind Spain's pastries and sweet dishes are tales of conquistadors, Aztecs, Moors and nuns. Chocolate arrived in Spain from Mexico and was embraced immediately; the Moors brought turrón, an almond and honey confection, to Europe via Spain, calling it halvo (making it a relative of halva); and the convent nuns created such sublime sweets as tocino de cielo (bacon from heaven).

All around Spain, you will find wonderful regional pastries — from Santiago de Compostela in Galicia comes torta de Santiago; and from Catalonia, brazos de gitano (gypsy's arm rolls), a favourite on feast days. But the most celebrated of Spanish sweets is turrón, without which no Spaniard could celebrate Easter or Christmas. In the weeks before these religious festivals, stores fill up with boxes of turrón blando (soft), the turrón duro (hard) de Alicante, or the soft brown confection called pan de Cadiz. Although some say that turrón dates from pre-Roman times, it's clear to most food historians that it came with the Moors.

As did many of the sweets of Catalonia, such as the bisbalenc (a sort of strudel filled with sweet squash paste and topped with pine nuts and sugar) from the coastal Ampurdan region and panellets (marzipan balls coated with grilled (broiled) pine nuts). Very un-Moorish is the most famous dessert of the region, now on menus all over Spain: crema catalana (also called flan catalan). Unlike French crème brûlée, it is made with the addition of lemon juice and cinnamon.

But it is the nuns in the convents of Spain, especially in Andalusia, Extremadura and Castile, who are the keepers of the traditional sweet recipes. For hundreds of years, these recipes, based on the simplest of ingredients — eggs, sugar, flour, lard or oil, sesame seeds and cinnamon — were closely guarded secrets, as unchanging as the articles of faith. Many convents have their own specialities. For example, in Osuna, the Dominican Santa Catalina convent makes capiruletas, a heavy uncooked custard cream made with egg yolks, sugar, ground almonds and cinnamon. There are various convents where you can buy desserts called yemas, based on candied egg yolks, the most famous of which, yemas de San Leandro, were — and still are — made by the nuns of San Leandro in Seville.

Finally it should be noted that the Spanish don't tend to cook sweets in their homes, nor do traditional Spanish restaurants serve a great variety of sweets. At the end of a meal, you are more likely to be offered seasonal fruit, cheese or a product from the local pastelería. Those who insist on dessert when dining out will have to make do with the ever-present flan catalan.

crema catalana .... serves 6

THOSE UNFAMILIAR WITH CATALAN CUISINE MAY LOOK AT THIS DISH AND SAY, 'BUT THIS IS THE FRENCH DESSERT CALLED CRÈME BRÛLÉE (BURNT CREAM)'. A CATALAN WILL LOOK AT A CRÈME BRÛLÉE, AND SAY, 'THEY'VE STOLEN OUR CREMA CATALANA'.

milk	1 litre (35 fl oz/4 cups)
vanilla bean	1, split lengthways and seeds scraped out
cinnamon stick	1
lemon	1 small, zest cut into strips
orange zest	2 strips, about 4 x 2 cm (1 1/2 x 3/4 inches)
egg yolks	8
caster (superfine) sugar	115 g (4 oz/1/2 cup)
cornflour (cornstarch)	40 g (1 1/2 oz/1/3 cup)
soft brown sugar	50 g (1 3/4 oz/1/4 cup)

Put the milk, vanilla seeds and bean, cinnamon stick, lemon zest and orange zest into a saucepan and bring to the boil. Simmer for about 5 minutes, then strain and set aside.

Whisk the egg yolks with the sugar in a bowl for 5 minutes, or until pale and creamy. Add the cornflour and mix well. Slowly add the warm milk mixture to the egg and whisk continuously. Return to the pan and cook over low–medium heat, stirring constantly, for 5–10 minutes, or until the mixture is thick and creamy. Do not boil as it will curdle. Pour into six 185 ml (6 fl oz/3/4 cup) ramekins and refrigerate for 6 hours, or overnight.

When ready to serve, sprinkle the top evenly with brown sugar and grill (broil) for 3 minutes, or until it caramelizes.

Prepare the vanilla bean by scraping out the seeds.

Slowly add the milk to the egg mixture, whisking constantly.

Cook the custard until it is thick, ensuring it does not boil.

flan de naranja .... serves 4

THE ADDITION OF ORANGE MAKES THIS A REFRESHINGLY DELICIOUS VARIATION ON THE OLD FAVOURITE, CREMA CATALANA, OFTEN THE ONLY DESSERT ON A SPANISH RESTAURANT MENU (ALONG WITH FRUIT AND CHEESE).

caster (superfine) sugar	275 g (9¾ oz)
fresh orange juice	200 ml (7 fl oz), strained
egg yolks	7, at room temperature
egg	1

Preheat the oven to 170°C (325°F/Gas 3). Lightly grease four 125 ml (4 fl oz/½ cup) ramekins or moulds with cooking oil spray and put in a roasting tin.

Put 80 g (2¾ oz/⅓ cup) of the sugar and 60 ml (2 fl oz/¼ cup) water in a small saucepan and stir gently over low heat until the sugar dissolves. Increase the heat to a low boil and cook for about 10 minutes, or until the mixture is golden and smells like caramel. Divide the toffee among the moulds and swirl to cover the bases.

Put the orange juice and remaining sugar in a small saucepan over low heat and stir gently until the sugar dissolves. Increase the heat, bring to the boil and cook for 2 minutes, or until the mixture is slightly syrupy. Leave to cool for 10 minutes.

Put the egg yolks and egg in a bowl and beat with a wooden spoon until combined. Pour the cooled orange juice onto the eggs, stirring until well combined. Pass the mixture through a sieve, then spoon into the moulds.

Pour enough boiling water into the roasting tin to come halfway up the outside of the moulds. Bake for 15 minutes, then carefully remove the moulds from the water and cool to room temperature. Chill completely in the refrigerator (this will take about 2 hours). When ready to serve, dip the moulds in hot water for 10 seconds, then invert onto serving plates.

Add the toffee to the moulds, swirling to cover the bases.

Heat the orange juice and sugar until turning slightly thick.

chocolate y churros

Of all the foods the Spanish brought back from the New World (potatoes, tomatoes, capsicums (peppers) and chillies) none was more quickly and enthusiastically embraced than chocolate. There was a simple reason for this. The Aztecs of Mexico told the soldiers in the army of Hernán Cortés that chocolate was an aphrodisiac. Montezuma, the Aztec king, employed twenty women solely to prepare his drinking chocolate, often ceremonially served in leopard-skin cups. The Spanish soldiers observed that chocolate harvest time was accompanied by wild orgies.

But the chocolate drunk by the Aztecs was very different from the drink enjoyed at today's churrerias (chocolate and churros shops). The Aztecs spiked their drink with spices, ground flowers and chilli, and added achiote, a seed that dyed the drink red.

As you would expect, this dangerous drink was not welcomed by the Spanish clergy. Even when the aphrodisiac rumour was finally put to bed, there was argument over whether the drinking of chocolate broke the Lenten fast. Curious, then, that some time later, the bitter drink of the Aztecs was transformed by the nuns at a convent in Guajaca into the delicious concoction enjoyed today, simply by adding sugar. Later, it was accepted by and, indeed, embraced by the clergy — so much so that it became the favoured breakfast of the Grand Inquisitor, prepared for him by the nuns in his service — an ironic reminder of Montezuma's chocolate maidens.

Walk into a churreria on any morning and you will find revellers on their way home and workers starting the day sitting side by side, dunking their churros in chocolate so thick the churros stand up in it. This espeso (thick) chocolate is achieved by the addition of cornflour (cornstarch). And what is a churro? One of the frutas del sartén, a fruit of the frying pan. A flour and water batter is forced through a ridged pipe — which gives the churro its distinctive form — and then carefully piped into boiling hot oil, before being cut into edible lengths. This combination of chocolate and churros, with a small glass of aniseed liqueur, is perhaps the most Spanish way to start the day — or end the night.

CLAVILEÑO

churros and
hot chocolate . . . . serves 4

A SPANIARD WOULD BE PUZZLED BY THE INCLUSION OF THESE RECIPES IN A BOOK — THEY HAVE ONLY TO WALK TO THE CORNER CAFÉ TO BE ABLE TO INDULGE IN THIS EXTREMELY RICH LATE-NIGHT OR BREAKFAST SNACK. FOR THOSE OF US WHO ARE NOT SO LUCKY, HERE IT IS.

sugar	110 g (3³/4 oz/¹/2 cup)
ground cinnamon	1 teaspoon
butter	30 g (1 oz)
plain (all-purpose) flour	150 g (5¹/2 oz)
orange zest	¹/2 teaspoon finely grated
caster (superfine) sugar	¹/4 teaspoon
eggs	2
vegetable oil	1 litre (35 fl oz/4 cups), for deep-frying

hot chocolate

cornflour (cornstarch)	2 tablespoons
milk	1 litre (35 fl oz/4 cups), plus 2 tablespoons, extra
good-quality dark chocolate	200 g (7 oz), chopped
sugar	to taste

Combine the sugar and cinnamon and spread the mixture out on a plate.

Put the butter, flour, orange zest, caster sugar, 170 ml (5¹/2 fl oz/²/3 cup) water and a pinch of salt in a heavy-based saucepan. Stir over low heat until the butter softens and forms a dough with the other ingredients. Continue to cook for 2–3 minutes, stirring constantly, until the dough forms a ball around the spoon and leaves a coating on the base of the pan.

Transfer the dough to a food processor and, with the motor running, add the eggs. Do not overprocess. If the dough is too soft to snip with scissors, return it to the pan and cook, stirring, over low heat until it is firmer. Spoon the dough into a piping bag fitted with a 5 mm (¹/4 inch) star nozzle.

Heat the oil in a wide saucepan to 180°C (350°F), or until a cube of bread browns in 15 seconds. Pipe 6–8 cm (2¹/2–3¹/4 inches) lengths of batter into the oil, a few at a time. An easy technique is to pipe with one hand and cut the batter off using kitchen scissors in the other hand.

Cook the churros for about 3 minutes, or until puffed and golden, turning once or twice. Drain each batch on paper towels. While still hot, toss them in the sugar mixture and serve at once.

To make the hot chocolate, mix the cornflour and the extra milk to a smooth paste. Put the chocolate and remaining milk in a saucepan and whisk constantly over low heat until just warm. Stir 2 tablespoons of the chocolate milk into the cornflour paste, then return all the paste to the milk. Whisking constantly, cook the mixture until it just begins to boil. Remove from the heat, add sugar to taste, and whisk for 1 minute. Serve with the churros.

Pipe lengths of batter into the oil, snipping them off with scissors.

Whisk the chocolate mixture over low heat until warm.

higos rellenos .... serves 6

THE SEASON FOR FRESH FIGS IS SHORT AND INTENSE, BUT SO ABUNDANT ARE THE FIGS OF SPAIN THAT THEY CANNOT ALL BE EATEN AND, SO, MANY ARE DRIED. INGENIOUS METHODS OF UTILIZING THESE DRIED FIGS HAVE BEEN DEVISED, INCLUDING THIS SWEET, SYRUPY OFFERING.

honey	175 g (6 oz/^{1}/2 cup)
sweet dark sherry, such as Pedro Ximénez	125 ml (4 fl oz/^{1}/2 cup)
ground cinnamon	^{1}/4 teaspoon
dried figs	18 large
whole blanched almonds	18
dark chocolate	100 g (3^1/2 oz), cut into small pieces
thick (double/heavy) cream	for serving, optional

Combine the honey, sherry, cinnamon and dried figs with 375 ml (13 fl oz/1^1/2 cups) water in a large saucepan over high heat. Bring to the boil, then reduce the heat and simmer for 10 minutes. Remove the pan from the heat and set aside for 3 hours. Remove the figs with a slotted spoon, reserving the liquid.

Preheat the oven to 180°C (350°F/Gas 4). Return the pan of liquid to the stove and boil over high heat for 5 minutes, or until syrupy, then set aside. Snip the stems from the figs with scissors, then cut a slit in the top of each fig with a small, sharp knife. Push an almond and a few shards of chocolate into each slit. Put the figs in a lightly buttered dish and bake for 15 minutes, or until the chocolate has melted.

Serve 3 figs per person with a little of the sherry syrup poured over and a dollop of cream alongside, if using.

Each September, in the town of Lloret on the Spanish island of Majorca, there is a fiesta devoted to the fig. During this time you may try over 63 varieties of this luscious fruit and see the crowning of that year's Fig Princess. Walk anywhere in rural southern Spain during the summer and you will see trees heavy with the fruit. Enter any market and you can admire the bulging purple or green fruit laid lovingly side by side. When fresh, figs are eaten simply with cheese or slices of jamón. When dried, they are stuffed with everything from blue cheese to walnuts and honey, or packed into little cakes with bay leaves and fennel.

three ways with fruit

IN SUMMER, SPANISH MARKETS ARE FILLED WITH THE SCENT OF APRICOTS, PLUMS, PEACHES, PEARS AND NECTARINES, AS WELL AS MELONS OF EVERY SHAPE AND COLOUR. WITH SUCH A CORNUCOPIA OF FRUIT, IT COMES AS NO SURPRISE THAT FRUIT DESSERTS ABOUND. SIMPLICITY IS THEIR KEY, AS THESE RECIPES SHOW. THE FIRST OF THEM, PEARS IN RED WINE, IS A CATALAN CLASSIC; THE SECOND, GAZPACHO DE FRUTAS, IS FROM MAJORCA; AND THE THIRD IS A TRADITIONAL ASTURIAN RECIPE MADE DURING THE APPLE-PICKING CIDER SEASON.

pears cooked in red wine

Rub 4 peeled firm, ripe pears with 80 ml (2½ fl oz/⅓ cup) lemon juice. Put 250 ml (9 fl oz/1 cup) dry red wine, 2 cinnamon sticks, 225 g (8 oz/1 cup) sugar, 8 lemon slices and 250 ml (9 fl oz/1 cup) water in a saucepan over low heat and simmer gently until the sugar dissolves. Bring to the boil, then reduce the heat and simmer for about 15 minutes. Add the pears and simmer for another 20 minutes, carefully turning occasionally to ensure even colouring. Remove the lemon slices and leave the pears to soak in the syrup overnight, if possible. Remove the pears and simmer the syrup over high heat for about 15 minutes, or until it thickens slightly. Serve the pears whole, drizzled with the syrup. Serves 4.

gazpacho de frutas

Put 250 ml (9 fl oz/1 cup) Pedro Ximénez sherry, 250 ml (9 fl oz/1 cup) muscatel wine and 500 ml (17 fl oz/2 cups) of any other sweet wine you fancy (or use 1 litre (35 fl oz/4 cups) in total of the same wine) in a large bowl. Add 30 g (1 oz) sugar, 90 g (3¼ oz) strawberries, and some slices of peeled peach, nectarines, melon and plums — any summer fruit will do. Mix well, and leave in the refrigerator for 1 hour. Before serving, pour over a bottle of cava (Catalan sparkling wine). Serves 8.

apple pudding

Peel, core and slice 800 g (1 lb 12 oz) firm cooking apples. Put in a saucepan with 125 ml (4 fl oz/½ cup) rum, mix together and simmer until the apples are softened. In a separate saucepan, put 500 ml (17 fl oz/2 cups) water with 200 g (7 oz) sugar and heat, stirring constantly, until the sugar dissolves into a syrup. Add the syrup to the apples with another 125 ml (4 fl oz/½ cup) rum, 4 egg yolks, 85 g (3 oz) gelatine powder and 1 teaspoon lemon juice. Purée the mixture in a blender or pass through a sieve. Dissolve another 80 g (2¾ oz/⅓ cup) sugar with 60 ml (2 fl oz/¼ cup) water in a small saucepan over low heat, stirring until the sugar dissolves (without boiling), then increase the heat and watch carefully until it caramelizes. Pour into a long 1 kg (2 lb 4 oz) heatproof mould and swirl it around to coat the base and sides evenly. Pour over the apple mixture and cover with 6–8 savoiardi (sponge finger biscuits). Leave in the refrigerator for 8 hours or overnight and then turn out of the mould by upturning onto a plate. Serve with fresh cream. Serves 6.

tocino de cielo

TRANSLATED AS 'BACON FROM HEAVEN', THIS IS A POPULAR ANDALUSIAN RECIPE, OFTEN MADE BY THE NUNS IN THEIR CONVENTS. IT IS INDEED HEAVENLY, BUT ALSO SATISFYINGLY WICKED. IT IS TRADITIONALLY DECORATED WITH TINY MERINGUES, WHICH SIT ON TOP.

caster (superfine) sugar	280 g (10 oz/1¼ cups)
vanilla bean	1, sliced in half lengthways
egg yolks	6
egg	1

Preheat the oven to 180°C (350°F/Gas 4). Put 115 g (4 oz/½ cup) of the sugar and 2 tablespoons water in a small saucepan over low–medium heat. Stir with a metal spoon until all the sugar has dissolved. Bring to the boil and cook for another 10–15 minutes, or until the toffee is a rich golden colour. Remove from the heat and, taking care not to burn yourself, pour into a 20 cm (8 inch) square cake tin, tilting to cover the base.

Meanwhile, put 250 ml (9 fl oz/1 cup) water in a saucepan with the vanilla bean and remaining sugar. Bring to the boil, then reduce the heat and simmer for 10 minutes, or until the liquid has reduced to a slightly syrupy consistency. Allow to cool a little.

Using electric beaters, beat the egg yolks and whole egg until smooth. Slowly add a stream of the cooled sugar mixture while beating on high. Once combined, strain the liquid onto the toffee mixture in the cake tin.

Put the cake tin in a larger baking dish. Pour enough boiling water into the larger dish to come one-third of the way up the side of the cake tin. Bake for 30 minutes, or until just set. Allow to cool completely before serving. When cold, dip the tin into a hot water bath for 30 seconds to loosen the caramel. Run a knife around the custard and unmould onto a serving plate. Drizzle any remaining caramel over the top and cut into small squares.

Tilt the cake tin to ensure the toffee covers the base evenly.

Add the sugar mixture to the eggs, beating constantly.

Strain the egg mixture into the tin, covering the cooled toffee.

leche frita . . . . serves 4 to 6

MEANING FRIED MILK, THIS TRADITIONAL RECIPE FOUND ALL OVER SPAIN (BUT ESPECIALLY IN THE NORTH) MARRIES CINNAMON AND VANILLA. IT CAN BE FUSSY TO MAKE THE FIRST TIME, BUT IS WELL WORTH THE EFFORT — ESPECIALLY IF YOU ARE COOKING FOR CHILDREN.

milk	500 ml (17 fl oz/2 cups)
cinnamon stick	1
lemon zest	1 piece, about 1 x 5 cm (1/2 x 2 inches)
vanilla bean	1, split and seeds scraped out
unsalted butter	140 g (5 oz)
plain (all-purpose) flour	250 g (9 oz/2 cups)
caster (superfine) sugar	145 g (51/4 oz/2/3 cup)
eggs	4, separated
dry breadcrumbs	125 g (41/2 oz/11/4 cups)
vegetable oil	for shallow-frying
ground cinnamon	1 teaspoon, for dusting
caster (superfine) sugar	1 teaspoon, for dusting

Grease a 27 x 17 cm (10 3/4 x 6 1/2 inch) biscuit tin and line the base and long sides with baking paper. Put the milk, cinnamon stick, lemon zest and scraped vanilla bean and seeds in a saucepan and bring to the boil. Turn the heat off.

Melt the butter in a large heavy-based saucepan. Stir in 175 g (6 oz/1 1/2 cups) of the flour. The mixture will form a loose clump around your spoon. Stir over low heat for 30 seconds, then stir in the sugar. Gradually strain the milk into the pan, stirring constantly. Mix for about 10 minutes, or until a smooth mass forms and it leaves the side of the pan. Remove from the heat and stir in the egg yolks one at a time, beating well after each addition (the mixture should now be quite glossy). Spread the custard mixture in the tin, smoothing the surface with your hand. Set aside for 1 hour to cool and set.

Lightly whisk the egg whites together with a fork. Lift the set custard from the tin and carefully cut into 5 cm (2 inch) squares. Dip in the remaining flour to coat all sides. Dip into the egg whites, then the breadcrumbs. Set aside.

Add the oil to a large frying pan to a depth of 1 cm (1/2 inch). Heat the oil, add a few custard squares at a time and cook for 1 minute per side, or until browned. Drain on paper towels. Mix the sugar and cinnamon together and use to dust the squares while they are still hot. Serve hot or cold.

Add the flour to the butter, stirring with a wooden spoon.

Add the sugar and milk to the pan and stir until smooth.

Coat the custard squares in flour, then egg white and breadcrumbs.

three ways with citrus

THE BITTER ORANGE (TODAY KNOWN AS THE SEVILLE ORANGE) WAS THE FIRST ORANGE TO ARRIVE IN SPAIN, BROUGHT FROM CHINA BY THE MOORS IN THE TWELFTH CENTURY. SWEET ORANGES WOULD NOT ARRIVE FOR ANOTHER THREE HUNDRED YEARS. AN ORANGE GROVE WAS (AND STILL IS) PLANTED OUTSIDE THE ANCIENT MOSQUE, THE MESQUITA, IN CÓRDOBA, PROVIDING COLOUR, FRAGRANCE AND THIRST-SLAKING FRUIT TO WORSHIPPERS. LIKE MUCH IN SPAIN, THE FOLLOWING RECIPES STRADDLE THE ANCIENT AND MODERN.

bizcocho

Preheat the oven to 160°C (315°F/Gas 2–3). Using electric beaters, beat 6 eggs (at room temperature) and 375 g (13 oz) caster (superfine) sugar for 15 minutes, or until light and creamy. Beat in 2 teaspoons lemon zest. Using a large metal spoon or spatula, gently fold 175 g (6 oz/1½ cups) sifted plain (all-purpose) flour into the egg mixture. Lightly grease and line a 24 cm (9½ inch) springform tin. Pour in the batter and bake for 1 hour 10 minutes. Turn off the oven and leave the door open for 5 minutes, then remove the cake from the oven and allow to cool completely in the tin. Serves 8.

majorcan orange salad

Peel and cut 4 semi-ripe navel oranges into medium-thick slices and season with salt, white pepper (freshly ground if you have white peppercorns) and a little sugar. Finely chop the leaves of 2 mint sprigs and sprinkle them over the orange slices. Scatter with 100 g (3½ oz) good-quality pitted small black olives and add a generous dash of rich and fruity extra virgin olive oil. Toss and refrigerate for 30 minutes. Serves 4.

oranges with coconut

Peel and cut 3 Valencia oranges into 1.5 cm (⅝ inch) thick slices and arrange on a platter. Sprinkle with 2 tablespoons sugar and 60 g (2¼ oz/1 cup) unsweetened coconut flakes. Stir and allow to sit for 30 minutes. Add a dollop of thick (double/heavy) cream to each slice and serve. Serves 4.

bizcocho

gypsy's arm cake .... serves 8 to 10

BRAZOS DE GITANO, AS THIS RICH DESSERT IS KNOWN IN SPAIN, IS A FAVOURITE ON FEAST DAYS IN BARCELONA. FOR THE FULL SPANISH EFFECT, TRY PEDRO XIMÉNEZ FOR THE TEASPOON OF 'RICH SWEET SHERRY OR RUM'.

dark chocolate	200 g (7 oz), broken into pieces
strong black coffee	80 ml (2¹/₂ fl oz/¹/₃ cup)
eggs	7, brought to room temperature, then separated
caster (superfine) sugar	150 g (5¹/₂ oz)
icing (confectioners') sugar	1 tablespoon
cocoa	2 tablespoons
rich sweet sherry or rum	1 teaspoon
cream	300 ml (10¹/₂ fl oz), whipped

Preheat the oven to 180°C (350°F/Gas 4). Grease a 29 x 24 x 3 cm (11¹/₂ x 9¹/₂ x 1¹/₄ inch) swiss roll tin and line with baking paper.

Melt the chocolate and coffee in a bowl over a small saucepan of simmering water, stirring occasionally, until almost melted. Take care the bowl does not touch the water. Remove from the heat and stir until smooth. Set aside to cool a little.

Beat the egg yolks and sugar in a large bowl until light and creamy, then stir in the chocolate mixture. Whisk the egg whites in a separate bowl until soft peaks form. Using a large metal spoon or rubber spatula, gently fold the whites into the chocolate mixture. Pour the mixture into the lined tin and bake on the middle shelf of the oven for 15 minutes, or until the cake springs back when lightly touched in the middle. Turn off the oven and open the door slightly.

After 10 minutes, remove the tin from the oven and turn out the cake onto a tea towel that has been dusted with the combined icing sugar and cocoa. Leave for 30 minutes, or until cool.

Sprinkle the top of the sponge with the sherry and spread with the whipped cream. Roll the cake up, using the tea towel to help you, but removing it as you go. Wrap the cake in plastic wrap and refrigerate until ready to slice and serve.

Stir the chocolate mixture into the eggs and sugar.

Spread the cream over the cake, smoothing it with a knife.

Use a tea towel to help lift and roll the cake up.

torta de santiago .... serves 8

SINCE MEDIEVAL TIMES THE GALICIAN CITY OF SANTIAGO DE COMPOSTELA, IN SPAIN'S FAR NORTHWEST, HAS BEEN THE DESTINATION FOR THE MILLIONS OF PILGRIMS THAT HAVE WALKED THE PILGRIM'S WAY, STARTING FROM EITHER NAVARRA OR SOUTHERN FRANCE. AT THE END OF THEIR JOURNEY, THIS CAKE AWAITS THEM.

blanched whole almonds	450 g (1 lb), lightly roasted
unsalted butter	150 g (5½ oz), softened
caster (superfine) sugar	400 g (14 oz/1¾ cups)
eggs	6
plain (all-purpose) flour	150 g (5½ oz/1¼ cups)
lemon zest	2 teaspoons grated
lemon juice	2 tablespoons
icing (confectioners') sugar	for dusting

Preheat the oven to 170°C (325°F/Gas 3). Lightly grease a 24 cm (9½ inch) springform cake tin. Put the almonds in a food processor and grind until fine.

Using electric beaters, cream the butter and sugar in a bowl until light and fluffy. Add the eggs one at a time, beating well after each addition. Using a metal spoon, fold in the flour, ground almonds and the lemon zest. Stir until just combined and smooth.

Pour the batter into the prepared cake tin and bake for 1 hour 20 minutes, or until a skewer inserted in the centre comes out clean. Cool for 5 minutes, then brush the top with lemon juice. Transfer to a wire rack and cool completely. Dust with icing sugar in a cross pattern, using a stencil if you wish.

In early spring, the plains outside Palma, the capital of Majorca, are a sea of white almond blossom. Majorca is one of the major Spanish producers of almonds, which, although introduced to Spain by the Moors, were not extensively planted on the island until the eighteenth century. Each year, in early August, the nuts are shaken to the ground, the tough green skins cut off and the kernels left to dry in the sun before being sent for roasting or cracking. Today, mostly the soft-shelled varieties are farmed, but, if you look carefully, you can still find the more flavoursome, if more difficult to open, hard-shelled almonds in specialist nut shops.

three ways with dessert sherry

THE SINGLE-VARIETY DESSERT SHERRIES MADE FROM EITHER PEDRO XIMÉNEZ OR MUSCAT GRAPES ARE ONLY NOW BEING DISCOVERED BY THE OUTSIDE WORLD. THEY ARE A REVELATION, CONTAINING THE DEPTH AND LAYERS OF SHERRY, BUT WITH AN ADDED RICH SWEETNESS. THIS RENEWED POPULARITY IS FORTUNATE, AS, NOT LONG AGO, IT WAS SAID THAT THE PEDRO XIMÉNEZ GRAPE WAS NEARING EXTINCTION. TODAY, WINE LOVERS AND CHEFS ARE DISCOVERING THE VERSATILITY AND DELIGHTS OF THESE SHERRIES, IN COOKING AND FOR DRINKING.

torrijas

Dip both sides of 4 thick slices of day-old bread in 150–200 ml (5–7 fl oz) single-variety dessert sherry, then drizzle over any leftover liquid. Allow the bread to sit for a few minutes to absorb the sherry. Heat 60 ml (2 fl oz/1/4 cup) olive oil in a frying pan over medium heat. Beat 2 eggs with a dash of milk, then dip the bread slices into the egg. Fry the bread on each side for 3–4 minutes, or until golden brown. Drain on paper towels, then dust with 1 teaspoon ground cinnamon mixed with 2 tablespoons caster (superfine) sugar or, if you prefer, drizzle with honey. Serves 4.

drunken cakes

Cut 1 bizcocho (page 175), baked in a square or rectangular tin, into squares. Put 115 g (4 oz/1/2 cup) caster (superfine) sugar and 125 ml (4 fl oz/1/2 cup) water in a small saucepan over low heat and stir with a metal spoon until the sugar has dissolved. Bring to the boil for 4 minutes. Add 125 ml (4 fl oz/1/2 cup) single-variety dessert sherry and boil for 3 minutes, or until syrupy. Drizzle the syrup evenly over the cake squares. Dust the tops with ground cinnamon and serve with whipped cream. Serves 8–10.

pedro ximénez with chocolate

Rich, dark and exquisite, Pedro Ximénez sherry (pronounced 'shimeneth') is largely unknown in the non-Spanish world. Mysterious and exotic, it has a secret of its own: it loves chocolate. Pour it over chocolate ice cream or a chocolate pudding, add it to a recipe for chocolate cake, soak lightly stewed plums in it and eat them with something chocolate and, in winter, add it to hot chocolate. Now you know.

polvorones .... makes 20

THIS DISH TAKES ITS NAME FROM THE WORD *POLVO*, MEANING POWDER — THEY ARE VERY FRAGILE, AND BURST DELIGHTFULLY IN THE MOUTH AS YOU EAT THEM. POLVORONES ARE ANOTHER SPANISH SWEET THAT COMES INTO ITS OWN AT CHRISTMAS AND EASTER.

plain (all-purpose) flour	250 g (9 oz/2 cups), sifted
ground aniseed	1/2 teaspoon
icing (confectioners') sugar	125 g (4 1/2 oz/1 cup), sifted
butter	250 g (9 oz), softened
egg yolk	1
lemon juice	1 teaspoon
dry sherry	2 teaspoons

In a large bowl combine the flour, aniseed, 1 tablespoon of the icing sugar and a pinch of salt.

Beat the butter with electric beaters until pale and creamy, then beat in the egg yolk, lemon juice and sherry until well combined. Beat in half the flour mixture with the electric beaters, then stir in the remaining flour with a wooden spoon. Gather the dough into a ball with your hands, cover with plastic wrap and refrigerate for 1 hour. Preheat the oven to 150°C (300°F/Gas 2).

Roll out the dough on a floured surface to 1 cm (1/2 inch) thick. Using a 5 cm (2 inch) cutter, cut into cookies. Transfer to an ungreased baking sheet and bake for 20 minutes, or until the cookies are light brown and firm. Allow to cool slightly, then roll the cookies in the remaining icing sugar. Reserve any remaining icing sugar. Cool completely, then roll in the icing sugar again. Store the cookies, covered with any remaining icing sugar, for up to 2 weeks in an airtight container.

Stir in the last of the flour mixture to make a dough.

Use a dough cutter to cut out rounds of pastry.

Bake the cookies, then roll them in sugar, coating all over.

aniseed biscuits .... makes 16

THESE SIMPLE BISCUITS ARE MADE MORE INTRIGUING WITH THE ADDITION OF ANISEED, WHICH GIVES THEM A SWEET LIQUORICE EDGE. THEY ARE GOOD AT ANY TIME OF THE DAY AND WOULD MAKE A DELICIOUS ACCOMPANIMENT TO A CARAJILLO, A SHORT BLACK COFFEE LACED WITH ANISE.

plain (all-purpose) flour	375 g (13 oz/3 cups)
olive oil	125 ml (4 fl oz/1/2 cup)
beer	125 ml (4 fl oz/1/2 cup)
anisette liqueur	60 ml (2 fl oz/1/4 cup)
caster (superfine) sugar	115 g (4 oz/1/2 cup)
sesame seeds	40 g (11/2 oz/1/4 cup)
aniseeds	2 tablespoons

Preheat the oven to 200°C (400°F/Gas 6). Lightly grease a baking tray and line with baking paper.

Sift the flour and 1 teaspoon salt into a large bowl and make a well. Add the oil, beer and anisette liqueur and mix with a large metal spoon until the dough comes together. Transfer to a lightly floured surface and knead for about 3–4 minutes, or until smooth. Divide the dough in half, then divide each half into 8 portions.

In a small bowl, combine the sugar, sesame seeds and aniseeds.

Make a small pile of the seed mixture on a work surface and roll out each portion of dough over the mixture to a 15 cm (6 inch) round, embedding the seeds underneath. Put the rounds on the baking tray, with the seeds on top, and cook for 5–6 minutes, or until the bases are crisp. Put the biscuits under a grill (broiler) for about 40 seconds, or until the sugar caramelizes and the surface is golden. Transfer to a wire rack to cool.

Although aniseed is an important ingredient in some desserts, it is more often seen as a liqueur in Spain, as anise. When you see old men sitting around in cafés in the villages, they will, more than likely, have a small glass of anise in front of them. Although each region has its speciality — in Majorca, for example, they add aromatic herbs like rosemary and fennel to make a drink called hierbas — there are also the national brands. Perhaps the most famous of these are Chinchón (named after the town near Madrid) and Anis del Mono.

magdalenas

Every afternoon, Spanish school children run home to their mothers for the merienda (afternoon snack), which will often feature a few of these little cakes. Similarly, when they visit their abuelas (grandmothers), the first thing they will be given is a handful of magdalenas. This delicious little cake, here made using olive oil and a little lemon zest, is as much a part of the childhood memories of most Spaniards as the madeleine (a close relation) was for Marcel Proust, whose book Remembrance of Things Past, was famously provoked by the aroma of the little cake dipped in tea.

Magdalenas are another example, like the tortilla, of the 'direct and simple' school of Spanish culinary art. They are also, again like the tortilla, difficult to perfect. This recipe will help you in your attempts.

Preheat the oven to 190°C (375°F/Gas 5). Mix 225 g (8 oz/1¾ cups) plain (all-purpose) flour, 100 g (3½ oz/heaped ⅓ cup) caster (superfine) sugar and the grated zest of 1 lemon together in a bowl. Add 2 tablespoons milk, 200 ml (7 fl oz) olive oil and 6 egg yolks. Mix until smooth. In a separate bowl, whisk 6 egg whites until stiff, then add half to the olive oil mixture and beat in. Add the remaining beaten egg whites and mix thoroughly until smooth. Spoon the mixture into a greased 12-hole mini loaf tin or muffin tin and bake them in the oven for 20–25 minutes. Serve warm, straight from the oven. They will collapse slightly as they cool. Makes 12.

almond turrón
ice cream .... serves 6

THIS IS A COOL SUMMER VERSION OF TURRÓN, WHICH, IF THE MOORS DIDN'T THINK OF, THEY CERTAINLY SHOULD
HAVE. USE PEDRO XIMÉNEZ OR MUSCATEL SHERRY IN THE RECIPE IF YOU CAN.

caster (superfine) sugar	115 g (4 oz/$\frac{1}{2}$ cup)
blanched almonds	50 g (1$\frac{3}{4}$ oz/$\frac{1}{3}$ cup), roasted
egg yolks	6
caster (superfine) sugar	80 g (2$\frac{3}{4}$ oz/$\frac{1}{3}$ cup), extra
sweet sherry	100 ml (3$\frac{1}{2}$ fl oz)
cream	435 ml (15 fl oz/1$\frac{3}{4}$ cups)

To make the almond praline, combine the sugar and 60 ml (2 fl oz/ $\frac{1}{4}$ cup) water in a saucepan. Stir over low heat with a metal spoon until the sugar has dissolved. Increase the heat, bring to the boil and cook for 6 minutes, or until the mixture is dark golden brown (but not burnt). Scatter the almonds onto a greased baking tray, then pour on the toffee and set aside to harden.

Mix the egg yolks and sugar in a bowl with an electric beater until pale and creamy. Whisk in the sherry. Transfer the custard to a heatproof bowl over a saucepan of simmering water, making sure the bowl does not touch the water. Whisk constantly for about 12 minutes, or until the custard is thick and foamy. Remove from the heat at this point, cover and leave to cool.

Whip the cream until firm, but not stiff. When the custard is cool, gently fold in the cream using a large metal spoon or spatula until combined. Pour the mixture into a shallow metal container such as a cake tin with a 1 litre (35 fl oz/4 cups) capacity. Chill until frozen around the edges. Tip into a bowl and beat with an electric beater until smooth. Tip the custard back into the container and refreeze. Repeat this process three times, or until the ice cream is soft.

Crush the praline and fold it through the ice cream after the final mixing. For the final freezing, put the ice cream in an airtight container and cover with a piece of greaseproof paper and a lid. Freeze for at least 3 hours, or until set.

To make the praline, pour the hot toffee over the almonds.

Set the custard over simmering water and whisk until thick.

Beat the chilled ice cream until smooth, then refreeze it.

index

ajo blanco 104
albóndigas 22
alcachofas en vinagreta aromática 17
allioli 49
almond turrón ice cream 189
anchovies on toast 80
andalusian salmon in orange sauce 87
andrajos 150
aniseed biscuits 184
apple pudding 168

bacalao 63
bacalao with red capsicum 61
baked bream with capsicum, chilli and
    potatoes 79
banderillas 43
biscuits
    aniseed 184
    magdalenas 187
    polvorones 183
bizcocho 175
braised tuna 75
brazos de gitano 176
bream, baked, with capsicum, chilli and
    potatoes 79
broad beans with jamón 36
buñuelos de bacalao 39

cakes
    bizcocho 175
    drunken cakes 180
    gypsy's arm cake 176
    torta de santiago 179
calamari
    calamares fritos 43
    calamares a la plancha 47
    rice with stuffed squid 72
caldereta del condado 117
caldo gallego 109
capsicums 31
    baked bream with capsicum, chilli and
        potatoes 79
    marinated 31
    pimientos rellenos 153
    red capsicum salad 31
    spanish vegetable stew 31
catalan-style cannelloni 138
champiñones al ajillo 25
chicken 122

chicken cooked with beer 122
chicken in garlic sauce 36
chicken in saffron stew 133
chicken with raisins and pine nuts 134
chicken with samfaina sauce 122
cocido madrileño 110
pollo al chilindrón 126
pollo relleno 122
chickpeas 20, 113
    chickpeas with chorizo 20
    chickpeas and silverbeet 113
    cocido madrileño 110
    tripe with chickpeas 121
chilli olives 14
chocolate 157
    chocolate y churros 162
    churros and hot chocolate 164
    pedro ximénez with chocolate 180
chorizo
    chickpeas with chorizo 20
    chorizo in apple cider sauce 36
    cocido madrileño 110
    stewed lentils with chorizo 113
churros and hot chocolate 164
citrus 175
clams 71
    clams in fino sherry 68
    clams with white wine 71
cochifrito 118
cocido madrileño 101, 110
crab
    txangurro 97
crema catalana 158
croquetas 29

desserts
    crema catalana 158
    flan de naranja 161
    leche frita 172
    tocino de cielo 171
    torrijas 180
drunken cakes 180
duck
    pato con peras 125

eggs
    huevos a la flamenca 146
    scrambled eggs with asparagus 53
    tortilla 50

escabeche 83
escalivada 137

fabada asturiana 101, 113
fideus a la catalana 141
fish
    anchovies on toast 80
    andalusian salmon in orange sauce 87
    baked bream with capsicum, chilli and
        potatoes 79
    banderillas 43
    escabeche 83
    fish baked in salt 80
    fish sauces 86
    hake in green sauce 87
    sardinas murcianas 64
    skate with sherry vinegar 84
    suquet de peix 88
    trout with jamón 76
    tuna with tomato sauce 75
    zarzuela de pescado 91
    see also individual entries
flan de naranja 161
fruit
    apple pudding 168
    gazpacho de frutas 168
    higos rellenos 167
    majorcan orange salad 175
    oranges with coconut 175
    pears cooked in red wine 168

game 101
    pato con peras 125
    quails in vine leaves 129
    rabbit in red wine 130
garbanzo see chickpeas
garlic 25
    ajo blanco 104
    allioli 49
    champiñones al ajillo 25
    chicken in garlic sauce 36
    gambas al ajillo 25
    octopus in garlic almond sauce
        67
    pan con tomate 25
gazpacho 103
gazpacho de frutas 168
gypsy stew 114
gypsy's arm cake 176

hake in green sauce 87
haricot beans 114
   caldo gallego 109
   fabada asturiana 113
higos rellenos 167
huevos a la flamenca 146

jamón 106
   broad beans with jamón 36
   croquetas 29
   trout with jamón 76
jerez 18
judias verdes en salsa de tomate 137

lamb
   caldereta del condado 117
   cochifrito 118
   roast leg of lamb 130
leche frita 172
lentils, stewed, with chorizo 113
lobster in pimentón sauce 87

magdalenas 187
majorcan orange salad 175
marinated capsicums 31
marmitako 75
meatballs
   albóndigas 22
meat tapas 36
mushrooms 101
   champiñones al ajillo 25
   croquetas 28
mussels, stuffed 35

octopus
   octopus in garlic almond sauce 67
   pulpo gallego 58
oranges with coconut 175
oxtail stew 130
oysters, with sherry 68

pan con tomate 25
pasta
   andrajos 150
   catalan-style cannelloni 138
   fideus a la catalana 141
patatas bravas 26
pears
   pato con peras 125
   pears cooked in red wine 168
pedro ximénez with chocolate 180
pimentón 150
pimientos rellenos 153

pollo al chilindrón 126
pollo relleno 122
polvorones 183
pork
   cocido madrileño 110
   fideus a la catalana 141
   pimientos rellenos 153
potatoes
   baked bream with capsicum, chilli and
      potatoes 79
   patatas bravas 26
   russian salad 40
   tortilla 50
prawns
   boiled in sea water 80
   gambas al ajillo 25
   prawns with romesco sauce 44
   tortillitas de camerones 43
pulpo gallego 58
pulses 113

quails in vine leaves 129
queso 148

rabbit in red wine 130
red capsicum salad 31
rice 92
   rice with stuffed squid 72
   seafood paella 94
roast leg of lamb 130
russian salad 40

salt 80
salt cod 63
   andrajos 150
   bacalao with red capsicum 61
   buñuelos de bacalao 39
sardinas murcianas 64
scallops with cava sauce 68
scrambled eggs with asparagus 53
seafood 57
seafood paella 94
seafood tapas 43
sherry 18
   clams in fino sherry 68
   dessert sherries 180
   pato con peras 125
   sherry with oysters 68
   skate with sherry vinegar 84
silverbeet with raisins and pine nuts
   137
skate with sherry vinegar 84
sofregit 143

soups
   ajo blanco 104
   caldo gallego 109
   gazpacho 103
   zarzuela de pescado 91
spanish vegetable stew 31
stewed lentils with chorizo 113
stews
   caldereta del condado 117
   caldo gallego 190
   chicken in saffron stew 133
   cocido madrileño 110
   gypsy stew 114
   oxtail stew 130
   suquet de paix 88
stuffed crab 97
stuffed mussels 35
suquet de peix 88

tocino de cielo 171
torrijas 180
torta de santiago 179
tortilla 50
tortillitas de camerones 43
tripe with chickpeas 121
trout with jamón 76
tumbet 145
tuna 75
   banderillas 43
   braised tuna 75
   marmitako 75
   tuna empanadas 32
   tuna with tomato sauce 75
txangurro 97

vegetables
   alcachofas en vinagreta aromática 17
   champiñones al ajillo 25
   chickpeas and silverbeet 113
   escalivada 137
   judias verdes en salsa de tomate 137
   marinated capsicums 31
   patatas bravas 26
   red capsicum salad 31
   russian salad 40
   silverbeet with raisins and pine nuts 137
   spanish vegetable stew 31
   tumbet 145

wine 130
   and seafood 68, 71

zarzuela de pescado 91

This edition first published in Canada in 2005 by Whitecap Books, 351 Lynn Ave., North Vancouver, British Columbia, Canada, V7J 2C4.

www.whitecap.ca

First published in 2005 by Murdoch Books Pty Limited.

Design concept and designer: Vivien Valk
Project manager and editor: Margaret Malone
Text and additional recipes: John Newton
Recipes: Vicky Harris and Murdoch Books Test Kitchen
Food editor: Jane Lawson
Photographer: Ian Hofstetter
Extra photography by: Prue Ruscoe (chapter opener ingredient shots and double page spreads)
  and Martin Brigdale (location shots on pages 6, 9, 12, 56, 100 and 156)
Stylist: Katy Holder
Extra styling by: Jane Hann
Food preparation: Lee Husband and Georgina Leonard
Production: Monika Paratore

ISBN 1-55285-672-0

Printed by Toppan Hong Kong in 2005. PRINTED IN CHINA.

IMPORTANT: Those who might be at risk from the effects of salmonella poisoning (the elderly, pregnant women, young children and those suffering from immune deficiency diseases) should consult their doctor with any concerns about eating raw eggs.

CONVERSION GUIDE: You may find cooking times vary depending on the oven you are using. For fan-forced ovens, as a general rule, set the oven temperature to 20°C (70°F) lower than indicated in the recipe. We have used 20 ml (4 teaspoon) tablespoon measures. If you are using a 15 ml (3 teaspoon) tablespoon, for most recipes the difference will not be noticeable. However, for recipes using baking powder, gelatine, bicarbonate of soda, small amounts of flour and cornflour (cornstarch), add an extra teaspoon for each tablespoon specified.